Contemporary Catechetics Series

Prompted by many demands, a series of contributions to the "Writings on Catechetics" in the German publication, *Catechetical Papers*, now appear in book form. Selected for inclusion are those articles and essays of a particularly catechetical nature. The completed series of books will mirror the catechetical questions and problems of our day, as they are extracted from the "Writings" of the *Catechetical Papers*. Theoretical as well as practical themes will be chosen, in keeping with the aims and purposes of the magazine itself. This contemplated series will include essays on the development of new catechetical approaches, on the significance of Israel in religious instruction, and on the new insights into the teachings about "the last things," as well as on other pertinent catechetical issues.

FATHER JOSEF GOLDBRUNNER

Series Editor

THE USE OF
PARABLES
IN CATECHETICS

☦

Franz Mussner

Translated by
MARIA VON EROES

UNIVERSITY OF NOTRE DAME PRESS : 1965

226
Hymn

Imprimi Potest:

> *Howard J. Kenna, C.S.C.,*
> *Provincial*

Nihil obstat:

> *Joseph Hoffman, C.S.C.,*
> *Censor deputatus*

Imprimatur:

> ✠ *Leo A. Pursley, D.D.,*
> *Bishop of Fort Wayne-South Bend*
> *February 28, 1965*

Original German title:
DIE BOTSCHAFT DER GLEICHNISSE JESU
First published by Kösel Verlag, Munich, 1963

65908

FOREWORD

The greater part of the following interpretations of twenty-three parables of Jesus appeared in 1956 in the magazine *Catechetical Papers*. At that time they found such a favorable response that the author, encouraged by the editor, decided to prepare them for a second edition. They were slightly revised for this purpose, and seven other parables were added. May they serve to emphasize more clearly the message of Jesus, when brought to the attention of our faithful during catechism teaching or in sermons!

Helpful in a fruitful study of the following interpretations of the parables, the simultaneous use of a synopsis—containing the parallel texts of the first three gospels, printed side by side—would be most advisable, particularly for the layman. For this I would like to recommend the *German Synopsis* by Josef Schmid (3rd. ed., Regensburg, 1960).

CONTENTS

PREFACE

The Greek word for "parable" is *parabolé* and it is from this root that our word *parable* is derived. Literally, this Greek term means a "juxtaposition" in context with the word *parabollein,* the Greek verb, to juxtapose, to put side by side. This may help toward an understanding of what a parable is supposed to be. In a parable two things are juxtaposed: something taken from daily life or nature and a religious mystery, a religious doctrine, or a fact pertaining to the history of salvation (as for example the "kingdom of God"). However, in a parable the juxtaposition of a secular and religious reality is rarely brought out specifically because, typically, only the secular story is told which expresses the religious point in a figurative way. Therefore, a religious reality remains more or less concealed in the figurative theme of a parable, and it is left to him who listens (or to the reader) to recognize the lesson, the essential part, expressed by the tale.

Now something has already been explained which should be taken into account when a parable is interpreted, for the parable *delineates* a religious theme; but there is an important rule concerning interpretations which consists in the fact that, of the parable's figurative part, not every point is

1

translatable to the religious and redemptive reality, as with the rule applied to an allegory: a equals b. Rather, a careful analysis of the parable's meaning is necessary to bring out fully its religious aspect. In some parables the whole story only serves to clarify one single, salient point. In others, several points belonging to the figurative and essential part of the parable are emphasized which should then be juxtaposed. The reason for this is that there are few perfect parables to be found in the gospels because many parables, from the very start, were interwoven with allegorical features. Furthermore, there exists a possibility of interpreting quite a number of parables in different ways, according to the individual viewpoint. For instance, the parable of the Pharisee and the publican can be treated from the viewpoint of prayer (what should our mental attitude be when we pray?) or from the value-standard viewpoint (what is important in the eyes of God?). Then there are the so-called parables of double aspect containing a twofold lesson, like the parable of the prodigal son. It is therefore the peculiar nature of the parables which often causes controversies to arise among scholarly exegetes with respect to their interpretation and doctrine. However, there does exist a basic rule which, more than any other, guides the interpreter's aims, and that is the method of analogy, when applied to the rest of Our Lord's teachings, for we may well presume that Jesus teaches the same doctrine in His parables as He does elsewhere.

Moreover, according to the testimony found in the gospels the message of Jesus *cannot be separated from His Person.* As the promised Messias, whose eschatological and divine reign has already begun powerfully (compare Matt. 12:28 with Luke 11:20), Jesus definitely belongs to that very message itself. He is the Messianic Savior of the world. In public, Jesus probably admitted that He was the "Messias" only during His trial (Mark 14:61); otherwise, He forbade demons, those whom He had healed, and His disciples to call Him openly the Messias (Mark 1:24 f., 34, 43 f.; 3:11 f.; 5:43; 7:36; 8:26, 30; 9:9). But in a hidden manner Jesus certainly stated His position by using the mysterious title, "Son of Man"; or by pointedly revealing His authority as the antithesis of the Sermon on the Mount ("But *I* say to you"); or in His pronouncements soliciting followers ("Follow *me!*"); or by His miracles. For him who has ears to hear, this hidden jurisdiction claimed by Jesus can even be discerned in some parables as in that of the sower, the vineyard and the bad husbandman, the money entrusted to servants, and the ten virgins.

The parables of Jesus belong to the "primordial stones of tradition" (Joachim Jeremias). They still bear quite clearly the mark of their Palestinian background. They also reveal a master narrator of parables who loves nature and who, while observing men's daily lives and their actions sharply and critically, nevertheless takes an impartial view of life's occurrences. Jesus was able to hit the target unfailingly with the themes of His parables. But in many of these parables the related action suddenly turns to the unreal and at times even becomes incomprehensible (for instance, when the king praises the unfaithful steward), because for the sake of figuratively expressing the religious reality inherent, the story has to take this particular course. This statement should not be regarded as a criterion of later allegorical revisions; rather, features like the ones mentioned reveal precisely what Jesus really wanted to impart with His teaching. "Apparent disruptions in their context and divergencies in the flow of these stories are in fact Christological challenges" (Hoskyns); at least they are religious ones. The "improbable features" belonging to such parables distinguish them as originating in *Jesus!* In contrast, the "post-Easter" tradition tends to "normalize" them. Besides, Jesus is not the inventor of the parable as a particular form of religious instruction (see Isa. 5:1–7 [the cousin's vineyard]); the rabbinical scribes also liked to make use of the parable (see P. Fiebig, *Old Jewish Parables and the Parables of Jesus*). The paramount reason for using the parable as a form of religious instruction is the figurative presentation of a religious reality. This is what the Orient prefers, but concerning the teaching of Our Lord the specific reason for using the parable lies in His wish to obtain thereby either His listener's consent to faith or the hardening of his heart.

"And when he was alone, the twelve that were with him asked him the parable. And he said to them: To you it is given to know the mystery of the kingdom of God (the way this is brought out in the parable): But to them that are without, all things are done in parables: That seeing they may see, and not perceive; and hearing they may hear, and not understand: lest at any time they should be converted, and their sins should be forgiven them" (Mark 4:10–12; also compare with Isa. 6:9 f.). This means that, just because God demands something of men through and in Jesus, and this often remains concealed in the *parable*, they are thus given the opportunity to *consent* truly and freely to their *faith*. Those who have ears to hear and who accept the parable's message in faith recognize behind the story God's reality of salvation, His challenging demand. To him, however, who also has ears but does not wish to hear, it remains concealed; and therefore, the call for consent, coming from Jesus, does not touch him. And this remains valid to our present day.

The parables of Jesus have a long history of interpretation. It started right after Easter, when these parables began to be gathered and applied to the concrete needs of the Church. This process of including the parables in the evangelical tradition even led to the fact that in some of them certain figurative points received a more forceful and allegorical emphasis in the light of a particular story—as for example, their Christological allusions—but one should not overestimate this process of tradition. Or, parables which were originally addressed to the adversaries of Jesus were applied to members of the Church, so that in some instances this led to a more or less serious displacement of their doctrinal purposes, their salient point. For example, in the gospel of St. Matthew some of the parables, according to St. Luke and according to their specific content, were addressed to the adversaries of Jesus. This procedure served to eliminate the purely historical value of the parables, for in applying them to a new audience they received a new actuality in the Church. And furthermore, even the evangelists caused some parables to be interpreted in a quite specific manner by inserting them into a particular part and context of their gospel, e.g., into the eschatological discourse of Jesus (Mark 13, parallels), thus assigning them a new "place in life," namely, in the life and thinking of the Church. This evangelical way of interpreting the parables should by no means be minimized, though the interpreter will always have to make an investigation of the original situation in which the parable was told by Jesus.

The Church Fathers like to interpret the parables *allegorically.* Inspired by their faith, the compassionate Samaritan, for example, becomes Jesus Himself; and in the man dying in the ditch, half-dead from the wounds inflicted by the robbers, they simply see unredeemed humanity. This kind of interpretation of the Fathers certainly has its merit and nobody should slight it, but today we must first of all search for the true and original meaning of a parable, to understand clearly what Jesus intended to impart with His teaching. Modern interpretations try to do just that, especially since the publication of A. Juelicher's classical work about the parables of Jesus. However, even today, the interpretation of parables has not been terminated conclusively, and how could this be the case when we consider that the essence of a parable, as a *figurative narration,* lies in its ambiguity and complexity; and moreover, that the parables of Jesus participate in the inexhaustible and unfathomable fullness of *God's own word!* Much progress in this field, the interpretation of parables, has been made by the Englishman, D. H. Dodds (*The Parables of the Kingdom*), and by the German Protestant exegete, Dr. Joachim Jeremias (*The Parables of Jesus,* Goettingen, 1958). The author of the following interpretation of parables, which are primarily oriented toward their catechetical use, is highly indebted to both of these researchers, especially to the scholarly book by Jeremias, though he sometimes arrives at different conclusions in his work.

The catechetical importance of Our Lord's parables and their interpretation is obvious. Even in our technical age, they spell a singular charm for him who listens to them, for it is still Jesus Who, as the true teacher of His Church, stands before the eyes of the listener, and as always, these parables cause a decisive situation of either consent or refusal to arise once more, as referred to above. Thus the parables of Jesus belong today, and in the future, to the essential program of ecclesiastical instruction in the Faith.

THE SEED OF GOD
AND THE RESULT

A Sower Went Out to Sow
(Matt. 13:4–9; Mark 4:3–9; Luke 8:5–8)

To really grasp the lesson and significance of a parable, we must first of all consider its story or pictorial part very closely. Such an approach can be applied to the parable of the sower.

According to St. Mark, Jesus was at the Lake of Genesareth when He told this parable to a large crowd of people who had again gathered around Him. ". . . so that he went up into a ship and sat in the sea; and all the multitude was upon the land by the sea side" (Mark 4:1). And then Jesus began to speak to them "in parables" (v. 2). Among other things He told them the parable of the sower. "Hear ye:" He begins, and with this He does not wish to imply that His audience should pay attention as do children in school to whom one says: "Now, listen, all of you!" For this call of Jesus, His "Hear ye!" is addressed to the people of Galilee, that they might become aware of this hour of salvation which God granted to them. It means: "Consider carefully of whom I am going to speak and who is really meant by the sower." Later on we will come back to this call of Jesus, but first we will give thought to what Jesus has to say about the "sower."

8

The sower walks over the field and throws out his corn seed. This is a beautiful and familiar picture! Gravely and with great care, this man strides over the earth, a bag of seed kernels slung over his shoulder. Dipping his right hand into it, he scatters the seed over the field in rhythm with his steps. The "sower went forth to sow," and it happened that some seed "fell by the way side, and the birds of the air came and ate them up. And other some fell upon stony ground, where they had not much earth: and they sprung up immediately, because they had no deepness of earth. And when the sun was up they were scorched: and because they had not root, they withered away. And others fell among thorns: and the thorns grew up and choked them. And others fell upon good ground: and they brought forth fruit, some an hundredfold, some sixtyfold, and some thirtyfold."

A strange kind of sowing, we might well think! Why does the man sow by the wayside, on the poor ground, and especially among thorns? Why not only on the good ground? This is so because we are in the Holy Land! In Palestine the sowing is done differently; there, they sow first, and then the field is ploughed. Thus, the sower in our parable walks over an unploughed field. During the time of fallowness people had worn short cuts across the field, and on these paths the kernels fell and were easily seen by all the birds; and so, long before the ploughing began, they came and picked them up. Meanwhile briers had flourished, but now they are all shriveled and seedless, and so they are ploughed under with all their fallen seeds and the kernels of corn; later the thorns will shoot up again and choke the fresh young stalks of corn. Then again, the layer of humus is not evenly spread; in some places it is very thin, and right below there is hard rock, so that the seed cannot sink into deep ground, and the burning sun of the south will therefore scorch the delicate, little plants. Apparently the sower has not much luck with his work. But the rest of his seed falls on good ground after all, and there it yields rich fruit: thirty, sixty and a hundredfold—obviously an exaggeration used by Jesus. However, He is speaking in parables, and behind the exaggeration looms the religious truth: what He really means is the fruit of God's word which is able to grow superabundantly in the hearts of men.

St. Mark himself provides us with an interpretation of this parable (4:14–20) when he writes: "He that soweth, soweth the word." By that is meant God's own word—the gospel! And now we also know who the sower is of whom Jesus spoke in the form of a parable: it is He, Christ Himself. Jesus walks over the land of Galilee and sows the seed of His *word*. And His introductory call, "Hear ye!" is meant to direct the attention of His audience toward that hour of salvation in history which has already begun. For the sower, spoken of in this parable, stands in their very midst, and it is up to them to recognize this hour rightly so that the Lord's word may not be treated like those seeds of corn which fell by the wayside, among thorns, and on poor soil. Rather, the *word* is supposed to penetrate their hearts deeply, and there produce rich fruit, thirty, sixty, and even a hundredfold!

And what is the lesson gathered from this parable for Christ's disciples, for His Church? Have courage and confidence! In spite of difficulties, oppositions and failures, the seed of God's word yields fruit and, because God stands behind it all, even much more fruit than the ground seemed to promise at first. Neither a wrong kind of optimism nor a wrong kind of pessimism has any place in our lives.

THE KINGDOM OF GOD
IS MOST PRECIOUS

The Treasure and the Pearl
(Matt. 13:44–46)

According to the testimony of the evangelist Matthew, Jesus spoke frequently of the "kingdom of God." To elucidate the essential meaning of the "kingdom of God," its significance for men, and its comprehension by those who listened to His sermons, Jesus, the sower of God's word, preferred the form of the parable. The parables treating of God's kingdom include the treasure hidden in a field and the pearl found by the merchant.

"The kingdom of heaven is like unto a treasure hidden in a field. Which a man having found, hid it, and for joy thereof goeth, and selleth all that he hath, and buyeth that field" (13:44).

We will first take a closer look at the story of this parable. Perhaps the man spoken of therein is a poor day laborer who had been hired by a farmer. One day he is sent out to the field with a team of oxen to plough the seed into the soil. It so happens that, while ploughing, he sees a foreleg of one of the animals suddenly sink into the ground. The poor laborer goes to see what has happened and he cannot believe his eyes: from the dark hole into which the beast has fallen something seems to be gleaming.

He looks closer and reaches down. It is an old pot full of gold pieces—a treasure hidden in the field! Great joy fills the heart of the laborer, for now all want and misery, the steady companions of his life since childhood, will be banished at once. But how is he to become the owner of this treasure? Immediately he has a solution: he must buy the field at all costs and then the treasure will be his! Looking around cautiously to make sure that nobody has seen him, he quickly fills up the hole with his hands. When evening comes he drives his team of oxen home, trembling with joyous excitement. On the following day, much to the astonishment of his neighbors, he sells all his miserable belongings, and taking the proceeds to the unsuspecting owner of the field he buys it, including the treasure. Now his fortune is made!

And then Jesus immediately adds another parable: "Again the kingdom of heaven is like a merchant seeking good pearls. Who when he had found one pearl of great price, went his way, and sold all that he had, and bought it" (13:45, 46).

Whereas the story of the foregoing parable treated of a poor man, this one is concerned with a wealthy one, for the Greek word for "tradesman" in this parable indicated that he is a merchant. The wealthy pearl merchant passes through the elegant bazaars of a town where pearls are offered for sale. He is an expert in his field, and as he examines the articles spread out before him he scarcely believes his eyes for there, among the wares, he beholds a pearl which is more precious and more beautiful by far than any he has ever seen before! He knows instantly that this pearl is more precious than his vast possessions. The pearl has to be his, whatever the cost may be! He promptly secures an option for this pearl and, in a state of excitement, quickly returns home and sells all his property in order to acquire the pearl. He knows that now he is the wealthiest man in the world!

These are the two parables whose stories are told by Jesus in a few words. They are parables of the "kingdom of heaven" or the "kingdom of God." St. Matthew always speaks of the "kingdom of God," as was customary in the later period of Judaism. "The kingdom of God is like the two stories I have told you," declares Jesus. And in the presentation of these two stories we are able to recognize what Jesus intended to tell His listeners about the kingdom of God.

But what do we really learn from those two parables? Briefly, we learn something about the overwhelming joy which fills all those who have discovered that the kingdom of God is the most precious treasure, the most valuable pearl in their whole lives. It does not matter whether we are poor day laborers or rich merchants; that is quite unimportant, because the kingdom of God, should we discover it one day, will always be more precious and far more valuable to us than anything else. The joy of this discovery causes everything else experienced in our lives to seem quite unessential, even things which bring us great wealth or happiness, so that, from now on, the absolute abandonment of all that is most dear will be quite natural (Joachim Jeremias). Then, differences between riches and poverty begin to shrink and lose their importance when compared to the preciousness of that "treasure," of that "pearl," signifying the kingdom of God. Thus, Jesus wants to tell us that the kingdom of God is more precious and valuable than anything we might ever possess in our lives and that it will give us more than anything life could possibly offer.

However, what is *really* meant by the "kingdom of God," by the "kingdom of heaven?" It is impossible to express this in one sentence. The kingdom of God signifies the "reign of God." But what does this imply? According to Holy Scripture, the "kingdom of God," the "reign of God," really signifies the ultimate, the final stage of things to come, the very reason for all creation and the goal of history as a whole. Everything converges toward that end. In the works performed by Jesus, which were the hidden but powerful beginning of God's kingdom, we can best detect the meaning of this "kingdom of God." His miracles especially are signs which express the very nature of this kingdom if "seen" in the light of faith. It is here that we behold what happens through Jesus: "The blind see, the lame walk, the lepers are cleansed, the deaf hear, the dead rise again, the poor have the gospel preached to them (Matt. 11:5)." This is how Jesus Himself explained His works in using the words spoken by the great Isaias, who prophesied the coming of that time of salvation (compare Isa. 35:5 f., and

61:1 with Luke 7:22). And what happens here
through Jesus and His miracles? It happens that
all those things which burden the life of man, like
sorrow and need, sickness and death are eliminated
by God. Thus, the miracles of Jesus show us sym-
bolically what the kingdom of God, in its very nature, is supposed to be, namely, the elimination of
all that makes man's life so hard to bear and the
arrival of all that which represents joy and happiness for him: eternal life, sonship of God and eternal peace. Then the reign of the devil and of sinful-
ness will be no more and, in its place, there will be
the reign of God which would signify what Holy
Scripture is wont to call "salvation." In corres-
pondence with what Jesus and His Apostles revealed in this context, it would be a worthwhile task
to go through the New Testament, particularly the
gospels, with this in mind, that is, to establish the
true meaning of those passages alluding to the kingdom of God. This would lead to joyful and reward-
ing discoveries, as in the case of the day laborer
and the merchant quoted in our parables. And, at
the same time, the life of Jesus would be understood much better because it would be evident, for
example, that all the miracles which He performed
were "signs" of the future reign of God; that they
were in fact secretly heralding the arrival of this
reign in our own age. With such significant promises
as these and such a beginning it is possible to
bear life better. Also, it will prevent us from falling
an easy prey to false promises made by the fake
prophets of this world. Then we will be filled with

that tremendous, that overwhelming joy felt by the poor laborer and the rich merchant when they found the treasure and the pearl.

A RADICAL DECISION

The "Wise" Steward
(Luke 16:1–8)

At first glance this important parable is not easy to understand, and that is why we must consider its story content very carefully.

A wealthy landowner had employed a steward, perhaps even several of them, but we are not given any further information about this. One day the master is informed—by whom, we are not told here—that this steward is causing a good deal of damage by wasting his master's fortune, squandering everything recklessly and irresponsibly. The master calls for him and demands a strict accounting. In the story of this parable we must presume that the master concedes a certain time of grace to this dishonest steward until a successor comes to take his place. But the rogue uses this period to thoroughly deceive his master again and thus provide the means for his own further existence. How does he go about this? He calls his master's debtors together and arbitrarily cancels a great part of their debts. The one who owes his master a hundred barrels of oil receives a reduction of half the amount, and another one who owes a hundred quarters of wheat receives a reduction of twenty quarters. With regard to the value, this comes to about the same in both cases because oil is much more expensive than wheat. The Oriental loves to use high figures when he tells a story, but the tall figures of our parable have an additional purpose, for they emphasize the fact that the unfaithful steward is not satisfied with "pennies" to secure his future existence. And, this is precisely what he wishes to achieve with his dishonest manipulations, " . . . that when I shall be removed from the stewardship, they may receive me into their houses" (16:4), and then he will not have to beg and work. Without doubt, a very clever and cunning fellow! In spite of the additional injustice committed by the steward, the master, who of course hears about all this very soon, involuntarily praises his "wisdom," as Jesus says in His story. After all, one has to admit that he is a "wise" rogue! He gambles by placing everything on one card to assure himself the means of a future existence.

What happens further to this swindler is not told because Jesus, through this lesson, is bent on bringing out the *radical determination* of the steward to secure his future existence. With this parable Jesus tells us to go and assure ourselves of our future existence in the kingdom of God with just as much determination as the unfaithful steward had shown to secure his place in the world. But unfortunately, Jesus adds almost resignedly, this is not often the case: ". . . for the children of this world are wiser in their generation than the children of light" (16:8). Unfortunately those who belong to the world demonstrate far more radical determination to assure their earthly existence than do the children of light for their eternal one.

　　　Then the evangelist Luke adds another of Jesus' sayings to this parable: "And I say to you: Make unto you friends of the mammon of iniquity; that when you shall fail, they may receive you into everlasting dwellings" (16:9). Let us give separate thought to these words, without considering the context used by the evangelist in the foregoing parable. The phrase "mammon of iniquity" corresponds to an Aramaic expression and signifies a property obtained by unlawful means. What Jesus, however, implies here is all vile profit and we are to use this "to make friends." Why? Because of the judgment which God will exercise over us all! The "friends" we have made with our mammon are the poor who will then plead for us as our intercessors, as "friends" at the time of God's judgment. And so, we are now able to understand the reason which induced the evangelist to combine this saying of Jesus with the parable of the "wise" steward. For the lesson of this parable means: Go and provide decisively and radically for your divine existence in the kingdom of God! Then the gospel cites an example of how to go about this practically, namely, by giving sustenance to the poor with the help of our property which Jesus disdainfully calls here the "unjust mammon." Whoever helps the poor finds in them intercessors at judgment time and thus works decisively for his eternal existence. Because of this helping the poor he will then be admitted by God to the "eternal dwellings," that is, to eternal life. Thus he acts "wisely" during his earthly life like the bad steward in the story of this parable, who also provided radically for his future existence, though in a dishonest manner.

Just because of the incredibly drastic way in which Jesus tells us the story of this parable of the "wise" steward, He achieves what He wishes to impart to the "children of light": To act with radical determination in the things which belong to the kingdom of God!

AN EVENT WHICH CANNOT
BE HALTED

The Mustard Seed and the Leaven
(Matt. 13:31–33; Mark 4:30–32; Luke 13:18–21)

With the parable of the treasure and the pearl the Lord taught us something about the preciousness and uniqueness of the kingdom of God and the overwhelming joy which goes with its discovery. And now, with the help of two other parables we will be able to penetrate further the mystery of this kingdom. They are the parables of the mustard seed and the leaven.

The parable of the mustard seed, according to St. Luke goes this way: "He [Jesus] said therefore: To what is the kingdom of God like, and whereunto shall I resemble it? It is like a grain of mustard seed, which a man took and cast into his garden, and it grew and became a great tree, and the birds of the air lodged in the branches thereof" (13:18, 19). The introduction of this parable sounds a bit awkward but it corresponds to the rabbinical way of teaching, and Jesus frequently conformed to this method—which was generally used in His time—in order to make Himself understood by all people. The fact that the evangelist handed down to us this awkward kind of introduction proves that he was loyal and accurate to tradition. Now, we must refrain from translating the beginning of this parable the way it is often presented: "The kingdom of God is like a mustard seed . . .," but rather the way it corresponds to the rabbinical way of expression: "With the kingdom of God it is as with a mustard seed. . . ." This now serves to better clarify the essential lesson, the salient point of the parable, for what does Jesus really wish to tell us by the parable of the mustard seed? The parable's story brings this out distinctly. A man takes, so Jesus tells us, a tiny little grain of mustard and plants it in the soil of his garden. And behold, when it opens and shoots up it becomes a bush, about six to nine feet high (this is the height to which a mustard bush grows), and the birds can build their nests in its branches. Now this is a mighty contrast! In the beginning there was that tiny little mustard seed, scarcely visible; and in the end there is that huge bush! In the beginning, when the kingdom of God is "sown," it is small and insignificant, but when the Lord comes again everyone will marvel how great and mighty it has become!

Very similar to this parable is the one about the leaven which St. Matthew (13:33) and St. Luke (13:20, 21) transmitted to us. According to St. Luke it is as follows: "And again he said: Whereunto shall I esteem the kingdom of God to be like? It is like to leaven, which a woman took and hid in three measures of meal, till the whole was leavened."

A farmer's wife wants to bake for her large household a sizable quantity of bread which is meant to last for several days. She takes "three

measures of meal"—that is, about thirty-five quarts
—and with this she makes a dough, mixing in some
leaven to make it rise. Then she goes out to the
field, to work, and after a few hours she returns to
the house. And behold, the whole dough is leavened! Every housewife is familiar with this process. While the woman was gone, the leaven had
worked in the dough, quietly and inconspicuously,
till the entire dough was permeated.

So, Jesus announces, it is also thus in the
kingdom of God. As in the parable of the mustard
seed, the main issue is once more the contrast between the primary and ultimate phase of a process.
First we have but a small piece of leaven which the
woman places in the dough, and, in the end, the
whole dough is leavened. The same process holds
for the kingdom of God. First there is an insignificant beginning scarcely noticeable, with very little
hope for success. But in the end, when God's reign
becomes manifested to the whole world on the Last
Day, all will be astounded to see that everything is
"leavened" by the reign of God, and no one or no
thing will be exempted anymore.

Thus, in our parable the question does not
turn around the exterior or interior development of
God's kingdom during the course of the world's history. On the contrary, Holy Scripture leaves no
doubt that in the end, during the days of the Anti-
christ, only a small group of faithful will be left (see
the Apocalypse of St. John). What matters most is
the contrast between the primary phase which
seems so insignificant and hopeless, a carpenter of

Nazareth dying on the cross and twelve frightened and simple workmen from Galilee, and the ultimate phase, which will reveal the majestic power and infinite value of God's reign.

Now we understand why Jesus told these two parables at all and why they were included in the gospels. It was because the Church should know about this! For even the Apostles, in the face of their small numbers, their poor education, their lack of power and their human weakness, could doubt that any noteworthy success would result from their beginnings. They could even doubt that one day God would really be the supreme Lord and King over a world seemingly dominated by Satan, even though Jesus foretold this, as had the Prophets of the Old Covenant before Him. In view of the world's might and vastness, and Satan's dominion in it, they could have despaired of any accomplishment or definite success in their work. And this is not so very different today. God's purposes always seem defeated; the Church is more harassed and persecuted than ever; there never were so many martyrs as today! There are reasons enough for many Christians and missionaries of Jesus to lose courage. However, Jesus knew this; He had experienced the same kind of difficulties in His own life, for even His work seemed to end as a complete and catastrophic failure. And that is why He gave us these two parables of the mustard seed and the leaven, saying: "Have courage and be confident!" Even if my beginnings and activities in the service of God's kingdom as well as yours seem inadequate and hopeless, rest assured; ultimately God will be Lord in all and over all!"

Do these two parables of the mustard seed and the leaven contain a Christological allusion? In a hidden manner they certainly do! The mustard seed was planted in the garden once and for all, and only once was the leaven mixed into the flour, for *this was done by Jesus,* and whatever happens in the world through Jesus cannot be undone by anybody else. *An event which cannot be halted* had begun when He announced in Galilee the beginning of God's kingdom (see Mark 1:14). This is figuratively expressed in the parable of the mustard seed when Jesus speaks of "growth."

THE ENEMY AND THE
FAITHFUL COMMUNITY

The Cockle and the Fish Net
(Matt. 13:24–30, 47 f.)

We will first of all try to visualize the story
of the cockle and the wheat (13:24–30). A farmer
goes to sow wheat in his field. This reminds us once
more of the parable of the sower. When evening
comes he returns home, tired, but glad to have finished his work so that he and his family can lie down
to rest and sleep. But this farmer has a malicious
neighbor who has been enviously watching his farm
grow and prosper. He begrudges this prosperity
and thinks constantly of how he can hurt him. One
afternoon, while the "enemy" is watching his neighbor sowing his field, he has a diabolical idea: "I
will sow cockle in his field of wheat, poisonous darnel, which at first looks so very much like wheat.
Perhaps this will choke the wheat and, in any case,
it will cause damage and spoil his field of wheat."
Soon thereafter, on a pitch-dark night, when all
were fast asleep, he went out to the field of his
hated neighbor and speedily sowed cockle in the
field and "went his way." Nobody saw him. He did
not use the cockle seed sparingly and so, when the
wheat "was sprung up, and had brought forth fruit,
then appeared also the cockle." The farmer's serv-

ants were soon aware of this and, reporting it to
their master, they said: "Sir, didst thou not sow
good seed in thy field? whence then hath it cockle?"
Immediately the farmer knows from where this
comes: an enemy has done this! But, to the astonishment of his servants, he does not give the com-
mand to weed out the darnel, as is usually done; he
explains the reason thus: "No, lest perhaps gather-
ing up the cockle, you root up the wheat also together with it (13:27–29). This is a queer kind of
precaution which goes against the general rule. The
servants probably shook their heads and were perhaps secretly annoyed. "What is the matter with
our master?" they may have muttered. "This is
not the way a farmer acts! The darnel will surely
choke the young wheat; just wait and see!" But the
master persists and adds: "Suffer both to grow
until the harvest." Only at harvest time shall the
cockle be sorted out from the bushels of wheat, and
then it will be bound into bundles and used for fuel,
for in the Orient wood is scarce; therefore cockle
and the like are used as fuel, ". . . but the wheat
gather ye into my barns" (13:30).

Before we discuss the lesson of this parable
let us simultaneously consider the *parable of the fish
net* (13:47 f.), which runs parallel to the foregoing
parable of the cockle and the wheat. To fully understand the story of this parable we must, in spirit,
picture ourselves at the Lake of Genesareth in
Galilee, for it is likely that there on its shores Jesus
told this story. Fishermen were casting out their
large dragnets, as the Apostles often had done
before Jesus began to train them. The fishermen

begin drawing the net through the lake between two boats, gradually narrowing the circle until they finally drag it onto the shore. What a wriggling and squirming there is in that net of "all kinds of fishes," large and small, edible and inedible ones! Then the fishermen begin to sort the fish: the good and edible ones are put into barrels, but the bad and inedible ones are thrown away.

Every child can understand the story of both parables, for Jesus is able to describe facts clearly and picturesquely in a few sentences. But what about the lesson He wishes to impart with these two parables? They treat of the kingdom of God, which means that, through these parables, something of the very essence of God's reign is supposed to be revealed. To some extent the stories of these parables enable us already to realize what Jesus is aiming at. In the first parable the salient point is to be found in the harvest, in the second one in the separation of the fishes. Jesus wants to say: "At first God allows the wheat and the cockle to grow together side by side. Only at the end, at harvest time ('harvest' in the Bible signifies the Last Judgment which God will exercise through Jesus, His Messias), one will be separated from the other. Then the wheat will be gathered into the barn and the cockle burnt." And similarly, at first the good and the bad fishes splash around in the net and are dragged up to the shore; and it is only then that the sorting begins, not while they are being caught.

Here is an important lesson which remains valid for all times. Why? Because both within and without the Church there is a constant demand for a faithful community, free from all those who are only nominal members—Christians only by baptismal certificate and others of the same kind!

Why then does not God Himself see to it that the community which belongs to Jesus is realized here on earth, according to its true nature? Isn't such a thought a temptation for all those who are earnestly wishing to see God's reign established and who therefore often feel that the Church should treat all sham Christians in quite a different manner? For they say, this kind of Christian only causes scandal and thus makes the Church, in the eyes of the world, unworthy of acceptance. And those outside the Church are constantly saying: "Look at those Christians, the way they act! Are they supposed to represent the community of Jesus?" However, such an attitude would be against the essence of God's reign, says Jesus, for God works quite differently. He rejects the idea of the pure community which the Pharisees had already called for, and so He allows the cockle to grow quietly along with the wheat, and He suffers both the good and the bad fishes to be gathered in the same net. God will see to it that one day all this will be changed, but only when the time of "harvest" has come. Then the big separation will take place according to God's just judgment; then the great sorting out will begin. But not sooner. What Jesus wishes to tell us therefore with these two parables is: *"Be patient in the meantime!* Be patient like God. God will right everything in the end when the hour has come. For the time being, cast out your net as far as possible."

Thus both parables contain an important lesson about God Himself, imparted to us by Jesus: God is so patient and merciful that He allows both the cockle and the wheat to flourish at first within the community of Jesus, but being supreme and all-powerful, He can afford to take such a chance. The cockle will not choke the wheat. Both will grow until the harvest, which is absolutely sure to come, for all the fields are ripening. Then will God intervene to establish the pure community for the time of salvation. "Be ye patient," therefore, and learn to wait in the firm conviction that nothing will remain as it is now. The time of "harvest" *is* drawing near—this is a warning for the "cockle" and a hope for the "wheat."

There is one other trait in the parable of the cockle and the wheat which we must consider. Regarding the question posed by the servants, "Sir, didst thou not sow good seed in thy field? whence then hath it cockle?", the farmer in this parable answers: "An enemy hath done this." Here, according to the true religious concept, Jesus thinks of a definite enemy—the devil. That God's field of wheat is often so full of weeds is relevant to the mystery of iniquity. Not only God sows, but also the other one—Satan—sows too. If there has been much cockle in the Church at all times, this is not always her own fault. It is also the work of Satan. Whoever wishes to judge the Church and her history correctly must take into account that there also exists the "enemy" and, for the present, God only condescends to give him space and time.

GOD'S HELP IS CERTAIN
AND SPEEDY

The Pleading Neighbor and the Godless Judge
(Luke 11:5–8; 18:1–8)

Jesus spoke much about God, about His nature, His sentiment, His mode of being; and to illustrate this, Jesus preferably used the parable, as He did when He wished to teach men about the kingdom of God. Thus Jesus proclaims important doctrines about God in two specific parables which belong to the choice treasures of St. Luke's gospel. One of these parables is to be found in St. Luke (11:5–8), and is generally called the parable of the pleading neighbor or the parable on persistent prayer.

To get at the main point contained in this parable it is important to translate it correctly and directly from the Greek:"And He (Jesus) said to them: Which of you shall have a friend, and shall go to him at midnight and shall say to him: Friend, lend me three loaves, because a friend of mine is come off his journey to me, and I have *not* what to set before him. And he from within should answer, and say: Trouble me not, the door is now shut, and my children are with me in bed; I cannot rise and give thee. Yet if he shall continue knocking, I say to you, although he will not rise and give him, because he is his friend; yet, because of his importunity, he will rise, and give him as many as he needeth."

A man has an unexpected visitor, in the middle of the night, when everyone has long since gone to sleep. A friend, traveling through this place on his journey has arrived without announcement. There is much embarrassment, for that very day the bread was completely eaten and only on the following day would a fresh loaf be baked again. So the man cannot even offer his friend bread for dinner; and, even worse, this lack of bread bars him from offering hospitality, one of the most sacred duties of the Orient. There is nothing left to do but run over quickly to his neighbor, arouse him from sleep and beg him to lend him three loaves of bread, so that he may offer some to his friend who has arrived unexpectedly and hungry from his journey. The man knows that he can do this because he and his neighbor are good friends, and so he thinks: "I am sure my neighbor will not refuse me even if I knock at his door at this time of night. He will surely not say, Do not trouble me in the middle of the night! Rather, he will get up immediately and help me out by lending bread, and even if he will not do this because he is my friend, then at least he will do it in order to get back to sleep."

In telling this story, Jesus appeals to His listeners' own experiences: "Which of you shall have a friend . . . ?—for all of you have friends and know how they would act in a case like this. They would certainly not let you down but quite naturally would help you if you came to them with an urgent and justified plea, even if it were in the middle of the night. For this is the way real friends act toward each other; you know this very well!" But why does Jesus speak about a thing like this at all? Because this is supposed to be a parable which shows with how much confidence man can and should turn to God. Jesus wants to say: "If you come to God with an urgent and just supplication, then rest assured, He will quite certainly hear you, just as certainly as your friend and neighbor would. Your neighbor, as you well know from experience, will not respond in saying, 'Do not trouble me,' when you come to him asking for something, even if it is the middle of the night."

This parable therefore does not treat of the perseverance in prayer, as it is often misinterpreted, but rather of the *certainty of fulfillment*. God is to you that good neighbor and friend. That is what Jesus wishes to say.

God, however, fulfills our prayers not only with absolute certainty but also with speed. Jesus points this out to us in the parable of the godless judge (Luke 18:1–8).

Because in the underlying teaching of this parable God is contrasted with the judge, it is not the woman but the judge who stands in the center of the story. And the lesson Jesus wishes to impart about God is this: Though the judge in the story of this parable, who did not fear God and had no regard for men, finally obtained justice for the poor widow—in spite of her powerful opponent in this process—God in comparison will listen far more patiently to what His elect have to say, and He will obtain justice for them, not after "a long time" but "quickly."

Thus, Jesus teaches us in both parables something about God and His sentiment and, moreover, the attitude we should have towards God. We are to see in Him our friend and neighbor Who will quite surely and speedily help us if we call upon Him with full faith and confidence. But at the end of the second parable there is a word from Jesus which speaks of profound resignation: "But yet the Son of man, when he cometh, shall he find, think you, faith on earth?" (18:8), namely, the kind of faith which believes that God is in truth like this.

WHO IS MY NEIGHBOR?

The Compassionate Samaritan
(Luke 10:29–37)

The parable of the compassionate Samaritan is a classical example of the teaching of Jesus about our neighbor. In the introductory verses (10:25–28), the evangelist Luke informs us that one day a certain lawyer came to Jesus with a question designed to lure Him into a snare: "Master, what must I do to possess eternal life?" Jesus does not reply directly but poses a counterquestion, asking him what Holy Scripture has to say about this. Thereupon the lawyer promptly quotes two pertinent passages from the Old Testament: "Thou shalt love the Lord thy God with thy whole heart, and with thy whole soul, and with all thy strength, and with all thy mind (Deut. 6:5) and thy neighbor as thyself" (Lev. 19:18). Whereupon Jesus says: "Thou hast answered right: this do, and thou shalt live."

However, the lawyer wanted to "justify himself." But why? Had not Jesus just confirmed the fact that his answer was the correct one? But the lawyer is obviously not content with the approval he has received from Jesus. Instead, he tries to embark upon a learned discussion about Holy Scripture concerning this question, as was customary in rabbinical circles. For he quickly realizes that there is a problematic point in his own question, a point with regard to the conception of "neighbor" in the quoted passage from Leviticus. And so he continues to ask Jesus: "And who is (in reality) my neighbor mentioned in that question? What do you think, Jesus?"

Jesus does not reply to the question posed by the lawyer in the traditional manner of rabbinical doctrine, but with a parable, or a story as an example. "A certain man went down from Jerusalem to Jericho, and fell among robbers. . . ." In the Greek text the expression "he went down" is written in the imperfect tense, in the sense of "repeatedly," for this man went this way often, regularly and habitually. Because of the local situation, one may gather that this man who went down from Jerusalem to Jericho was a Jew. Jericho is situated about twenty-seven kilometers from Jerusalem in the ravine of the Jordan. The road descends about a thousand meters and leads through a desolate desert called Juda, interspersed with many gorges—quite a dangerous road to pass through even today. And so it happened that this time the man was felled by robbers. Now he lies there, on the roadside, seriously wounded, naked and half-dead.

By chance a priest went down the same way, also habitually, as the imperfect is used again. He was probably returning from his service in the Temple of Jerusalem, for Jericho was one of the priest-cities of Judea. He sees the half-dead and wounded man lying there, but he passes by without

bothering about him, and after a short while a Levite does the same. Perhaps the lawyer expected
Jesus to say in His story that the third one who
came along on that same road would be a lay Israelite, and so he probably could not believe his ears
when Jesus deliberately mentioned a Samaritan, as
the Samaritans were bitterly hated by the Jews.
And it is precisely this one who helps the poor man,
whereas the Jewish priest and Levite had not lent a
helping hand, though they could have assumed that
the wounded one belonged to their own race. And
now the Samaritan not only helps a little, but most
generously. He almost acts as though the stricken
man, whom he has found by chance, is his own son
or brother. And because of his helpfulness he becomes the "neighbor" of this wounded Jew. Jesus,
as might be expected, does not ask the lawyer at
the end of the parable, "Of those three men who
came along, who was it that saw in this wounded
man his neighbor?" But inversely, He asks, "Who
of those three acted like a neighbor toward the
wounded man?"

This point should be noted very carefully. In
thus formulating His last question directed to the
lawyer, Jesus touched upon the salient point in our
parable, the decisive center, the true *kerygma,* the
new and revolutionary aspect, in contrast to the
viewpoint of late Judaism, whose representative
stands before Him in the figure of the lawyer. But
how so? At the time of Jesus those who represented
"neighbors" among the Jews belonged to a very
small circle, far more restricted than originally in
the Old Testament. In the past, the transmitted

commandment from Leviticus (19:18), "Thou shalt love thy neighbor as thyself," was not only applied to fellow citizens but to a certain extent, also, to the "stranger," who "abides among you" (Lev. 19:33). But now, at the time of Jesus, only the Israelite and he who had completely proselytized, that is, only a member of the same race and faith, were accepted as neighbors, but not the heathen, and especially not the Samaritans who, according to their descent and also because of their cults and rites, belonged in the eyes of the Jews to the same category as the heathens. As we know from Flavius Josephus and the Talmud, the Jews called the Samaritans, "Cuthites," because according to IV Kings 17:24, heathen men "from Cutha" in Persia were brought to Samaria by the king of the Assyrians (in the year 722 B.C.) and settled there, where they intermingled with that part of the Jewish population which had escaped from being carried off to captivity. That is why the Jews denied the Samaritans the right to ascribe their descent to the Patriarchs; in their eyes the Samaritans were still heathens with whom it was forbidden to share the cultic rites and the common table. (See John 4:9, "For the Jews do not communicate with the Samaritans.") Characteristic of this attitude is the example of a well-known proverb stemming from the time of late Judaism: "Whoever eats bread coming from the Samaritans is like him who eats pork," which means that accepting something from a Samaritan, or even sharing a meal with him, is equivalent to apostasy.

It is important to know these historical and

cultural facts to understand the degree of anger
Jesus caused with His teaching about the "neighbor." For in our parable it is precisely one of these
hated Samaritans who helps the man who lies there
helpless, though he must be fully aware that the
wounded will regard him as his deadly enemy. The
Samaritan could have thought: "This serves him
right! At least he is one less!" But he does not think
that way; on the contrary, he helps him goodheart-
edly and generously. And so the Samaritan, as Jesus says, becomes the "neighbor" of the wounded
man—a fact even the lawyer has to admit, whether
he likes it or not—whereas those who were really
"neighbors," according to the Jewish point of view,
passed by on their way and left him in his misery.

     The lawyer had asked Jesus: "Who is really
my neighbor, according to your personal belief?"
The Lord replies in His parable that such a one is
not only your fellow countryman, but always any-
one who helps you in your need, though he be a
Jew, a Samaritan, a heathen, or someone else. Thus
Jesus completely upsets all views and doctrines ex-
isting up to then about the concept of "neighbor."
According to Him it is not the common bond of
blood, ancestry, and race (and consequently, also,
of education, religion or party system, and so on)
which makes one my neighbor; but rather, it is the
turning to each other in love which creates the bond
of neighborliness. Through this message of Jesus,
the concept of "neighbor" develops into something
which runs right through the whole bulk of humanity, cutting through all its natural and artificial

barriers and emancipations, thus overcoming all such restrictions again and again. And it is in this fact that we should see the actual importance of this parable, because there arises daily that tendency to primarily circumscribe and limit the circle of neighbors, and therefore to prevent the concept of "neighbor" from becoming world-wide in its value and forceful penetration, the way Jesus started and intended this to be. In all countries of the world we will find that teachings about our neighbors are being proclaimed wherever we go, but they are in sharp contrast to what Jesus taught about the "neighbor."

INVITATION AND CONVERSION

The Royal Marriage Feast
(Matt. 22:1–14; Luke 14:16–24)

The text of the parable of the royal marriage feast exists in two versions, one of which has been given to us by St. Matthew (22:1–14), the other by St. Luke (14:16–24). In the latter version the marriage feast is only mentioned as a "great supper." We are going to base the following interpretation on the text of St. Matthew because his paraenetical (Greek word for "utilization") rendition always remains applicable to the Church.

The kingdom of heaven is likened to a king, who made a marriage for his son. From this stereotyped introduction one should not draw the conclusion that Jesus "likened" or compared the kingdom of God to a king, for the whole story which Jesus tells us about this king only serves to illustrate allegorically what God's reign is really like.

How does the story of this parable go? A king wants to arrange, in the near future, a marriage for his son, the heir and successor of his throne. All invitations have long since been sent out to those who are to be present as guests at this marriage feast. But behold, when the chosen guests, according to Oriental custom, were asked

by the king's servants to accept the invitation, now
that the day of marriage was drawing near, "they
would not come"; and even when the king orders
his invitation to be repeated urgently—something
no other king would ever have done—he hears, to
his surprise, that the chosen guests are not at all
interested in his invitation, that they neglect his
call and prefer to go about their own business. Some
are even so indignant and irritated about this invitation that they badly mistreat the servants sent by
the king and even kill several of them. Of course,
this is a rather strange and quite incredible kind of
behavior, but concealed behind the story of this parable looms a profound truth of salvation, and that
is what influences the form of this tale. For Jesus
does not tell us just any kind of story, but a very
particular one in which both His listeners and He
Himself are deeply involved. But let us first return
to the story of our parable. As might be expected,
the king is outraged by the bad behavior of these
guests who were invited to his son's marriage, a
behavior which even goes beyond an offense against
sovereignty. The king sends his armies to destroy
the murderers of his servants and to burn their
city. And in place of those who were first invited,
who "were not worthy," he commands that others
should be called to the marriage—whomsoever his
servants may find at the crossroads and on the
highways "both bad and good: and the marriage
was filled with guests"(v. 10).

Now, the story of this parable could end here
and the lesson drawn therefrom would imply: *Ac-*

cept the invitation, namely, the invitation to enter into the kingdom of God, for eternal life. If you do not accept and come you will fare badly, and others will take your place. This parable warns of the future judgment of those who were first invited.

As we said before, the story of this parable is linked to the concrete facts of salvation, that is, coming from the mouth of Jesus, this parable was supposed to be a warning for Israel not to reject the proffered invitation to participate in the "banquet" of God's kingdom. If you refuse, you will be subjected to God's judgment. It is possible, but not certain, that the Prophets—and even Jesus Himself—were meant by the "servants" in this parable's story, but this is not essential for its comprehension, though it may round out the tale. Of course, the Christian reader believes the king's "son" to be Jesus and the "servants" to be the Prophets who were persecuted and killed by the Jews, and he may think of the "city" as Jerusalem and of the events which occurred in the year 70 A.D. (compare this with the parable of the wicked tenants of the vineyard). Perhaps, later on, these happenings had a certain influence on the formulation of the text, but what remains remarkable is that those who were invited to the feast in place of the murderers were not called heathens but, in general, "bad and good."

Verse 10 could very well end our parable, but its story proceeds just as the marriage feast is about to start. The king enters the banquet hall to see his guests. There he discovers a man who has no wedding garment. And when the king confronts him, the man is "silent," conscious of his guilt. He had not deemed it necessary to first go home and clothe himself with a garment worthy of the occasion, and only then to enter the banquet hall. This man had come exactly as he was, from the street, and had seated himself at the royal banquet. While the refusal of those who had been chosen to accept the invitation to the feast was an offense against the sovereign (and even more than that), the improper garb of this man is now equally disrespectful. "Then the king said to the waiters: Bind his hands and feet, and cast him into the exterior darkness. . . ."

This is the second part of the story. If we inquire about its lesson, we hear this: *Woe to him who comes unprepared (without a wedding garment) to the banquet of God's kingdom.* He will be cast out from the banquet hall into the darkness of hell—again a warning of judgment. It is uncertain whether the wedding garment was meant to be something specific. Some Church Fathers thought that the implication was love (as did Gregory the Great); modern exegetes think it might mean conversion. One should also consider that, instead of those who were first invited, it is now the bad (the sinners) as well as the good who are called to attend. Overwhelmed by the king's mercy, these bad ones had evidently been converted or were given to performing works of charity, so that now they were able to endure the critical glance of his eyes; whereas, that other man did not think it necessary to make any kind of effort and dared to enter the banquet hall without a wedding garment, and so proved to be unworthy of partaking of the banquet.

Why, then, did the story not end with the tenth but rather with the thirteenth verse? The reason is that the first part of the parable might have caused grave misunderstanding among those who read it or listened to it. They might think the king to be so good that, in place of those first ones who were unworthy, he now simply invites all the good and bad taken from the crossroads to attend the marriage of his son. This might induce some men to conceive the disastrous idea that they do not have to bother about going home first to don a festive garment but that they are welcome the way they are at the marriage feast. "This is where you err," Jesus tells us, "for, without a wedding garment" (that is, without due preparation or adequate proof of worthiness) "nobody will be admitted to the banquet of God's kingdom. Do not deceive yourselves about all this!" That is why there is a second part to this parable.

The final (fourteenth) verse of this parable as handed down to us by St. Matthew seems to have been originally a separate phrase of Our Lord which the evangelist inserted here for the sake of once more preventing a dangerous misunderstanding of the first part of the story. Certainly, all men are invited by God—that is what is meant by being *called* —but the number of those who in the end will really partake of the banquet in God's kingdom will in no way correspond to the number of those who were invited. Many do not prepare themselves and thus remain excluded from His kingdom. Therefore, the number of those who really participate will be small in comparison to those who are invited. This is to be understood as a repeated and very serious warning against a "Church of the masses," where the good and the bad live peacefully side by side, at least for the time being.

WHO IS JUSTIFIED BY GOD?

The Pharisee and the Publican
(Luke 18:9–14)

Again let us first take a look at the story of this parable. Jesus tells us that two men "went up into the temple," and this expression "went up" is exactly what the local situation calls for because the mount of the Temple is on a higher level than the rest of the city. One of these two men is a Pharisee. Who were these Pharisees, really? To know this is very important for the right interpretation of our parable, as there exists quite a number of erroneous ideas in this respect.

The origin of the Pharisees goes far back into the history of the Jewish nation and is therefore historically undetermined. The Pharisees seem to have organized even before the time of the Maccabees under the name of "Hasidean," that is, holy, devout men. Then they appeared two centuries before Christ under the self-chosen name of Pharisees (which means, the select, the separate ones). In the last century before Christ they managed to be admitted to the High Council, that is, to the Jewish Government. They gained wide influence in religious matters mainly through the fact that the so-called scribes were chosen, for the greater part,

from the group of Pharisees. However, it is quite
wrong to imagine the Pharisees as a theological
school, a political-religious party, or even a Jewish sect. The Pharisees represented, rather, a lay
movement and a lay community, predominantly
formed by merchants, workmen, and peasants
under the spiritual leadership of the scribes. Their
group was a relatively small one. At the time of
King Herod (39–4 B.C.), there were about 6000
Pharisees in Palestine.

Above all, the Pharisee bound himself to the
voluntary fulfillment of additional laws of purification which were ordinarily kept only by priests.
The Pharisee also bound himself to the strict ob-
servance of the tithing regulations; and to keep
these rules was not an easy thing in daily life because all other citizens of that nation were quite
remiss about them; and therefore the Pharisees
were in constant danger of acting against the laws
of purification, for example, by buying untithed
fruit in the market and then consuming it in their
households. Thus they were forced to form an association called "Haburoth" which enabled them to
buy from fellow members and to eat with them
without scruples. But naturally this led to a complete separation of the Pharisee from other people,
and that is why they called themselves with pride
"the select."

But why did they bind themselves to fulfill
these exclusively priestly regulations though they
were laymen? This again can be traced back to a
commandment of God in the Old Testament: "And

you shall be to me a *priestly* kingdom, and a holy nation" (Exod. 19:6). To attain this goal the Pharisees voluntarily kept rules which otherwise were only observed by priests. In conjunction with this idea there was another one added from the Old Testament, namely, the one speaking of the "holy rest," alluded to, for example, in the Book of Kings (III, 19:18): "And I will leave me seven thousand men in Israel, whose knees have not been bowed before Baal. . . ." Now compare this to Isaias (4:3): "And it shall come to pass that everyone that shall be left in Sion, and that shall remain in Jerusalem, shall be called holy; everyone that is written in life in Jerusalem." According to the Prophet Zacharias (14:2) only a remnant will be saved from destruction at the final battle of Jerusalem. As Joachim Jeremias says, "This prophetic message of the holy remnant has influenced in a most extraordinary way the religious thinking of the world at the time of Jesus as well as determined the history of Late Judaism. This is why there were so many groups formed within Judaism who believed that they represented that "holy rest"—as for example, the Essenes, with whose ideas we are now much better acquainted since the discovery of their texts in Qumran; the Jewish community of the Therapeutes in Egypt; but particularly the Pharisees, who were upbraided by St. John the Baptist (Matt. 3:7): "Ye brood of vipers, who hath shewed you to flee from the wrath to come?" Moreover, Jesus definitely refused to gather around Him a select community who represented that remnant, as the parables of

the cockle and the wheat and that of the fish net
prove convincingly. He was far from forming a
clique, a group of select, of holy and devout men;
instead, according to the gospel, He turned to all,
and especially to those who had been primarily excluded from the kingdom of God by the Pharisees.
He turned to sinners, to harlots and publicans, and
that is precisely why He called forth the anger and
wrath of the Pharisees. The fact that they, "the select," the "holy rest," the "faithful community" were
called by Jesus to convert themselves, as the Baptist had called them before Jesus, was something
which provoked their irrevocable hatred and finally
brought Christ to the cross.

From the foregoing we must therefore con-
clude that the Pharisees were by no means what
one might call "crippled religious" as to their char-
acter. In reality, nobody in the Jewish nation was
more filled with religious earnestness and passion-
ate zeal for God than they. But the very nature and
method of their type of piety—their hardness toward those whom they deemed notorious sinners,
like the publicans; their subtle and shrewd casu-
istry which enabled them to avoid the lawful regulations (wherefore Jesus called them "hypocrites");
their doctrine of retaliation; their arrogance in face
of the multitude that "keepeth not the law" (John
7:19); and their religious formalism—led to the
deterioration of religion and caused Jesus to become a sharp adversary of Pharisaism. That so
many arguments between Jesus and the Pharisees
were preserved in the gospel certainly has its rea-

sons in the fact that the conflict between Jesus and
those models of piety was to serve as an eternal
warning also for Christians. For religion deterio-
rates primarily in the direction of Pharisaism! This
is also a latent danger of Christianity, and that is
why it is so important to clearly understand the essence of Pharisaism. Its history proves that in the
name of "piety" one may well become an enemy of
Jesus and consequently of God.

Who were the publicans? They were, as their
professional title indicates, men who collected the
tariffs imposed on articles which were imported or
exported. Therefore the publicans were not tax collectors in our sense of the word. At the time of Jesus
the revenues of tariffs coming from Judea and Samaria flowed into the imperial treasury, whereas
those tariffs which were raised at the borders of
Galilee and Peraeus belonged to the Jewish te-
trarchs, for example, to Herod Antipas, the gover-
nor of the district where Jesus lived. The publican
was therefore employed by the hated heathen
rulers who governed the country and also by the no
less abhorred family of the Herodians. Added to
these circumstances was the manner in which this
business of tariff collecting was conducted. The tariffs were not collected by state employees, as we
collect them, but by tenants who, for a yearly sum,
rented the entire tariff extracted from a certain
district, and then the collectors were allowed to
keep what amounted to a surplus of that specific
tariff. The sum raised by the tariff was prescribed
by the authorities but, because the tariffs often var-

ied, a wide range of profit was left to the arbitrari-
ness and avarice of the publicans. That is why they
were regarded as exploiters and notorious sinners,
not only by the Pharisees but also by all other people. You may compare this statement with the
text of St. Luke (19:7) where Zacheus, who was
a chief publican by profession, was simply called
"a sinner," and likewise the passage in St. Luke
(15:1) where the words "publicans" and "sinners"
are interchanged in the same breath. In rabbinical
literature the publicans hold the same rank as other
so-called notorious sinners, like tax collectors, robbers, moneychangers, heathens, harlots, swindlers
and adulterers. It was forbidden to use any money
taken from the publican's purse for the official fund
of the poor. If a man who belonged to the Pharisees
wished to make his profession that of a publican, he
was quite naturally excluded from their association
and officially deprived of all rights; he was fairly
ostracized. He could never become a judge and was
not even permitted to testify at court. He was simply regarded as a scoundrel because of his profession.

Now, in the story of our parable, Jesus lets
a Pharisee and a publican go up to the Temple to
pray, and only if we know what kind of men they
really were, are we able to understand this parable
correctly. We see the Pharisee walking with great
dignity through the outer courts of the Temple en-
closure till he comes to stand before the outer court
of the priests, face to face with the sacrificial altar.
There he takes a haughty position and says his

prayers. He thanks God that he is not "as the rest of men," thinking particularly of "this publican" —and the little word "this" reveals how utterly he despises the man—whom he had probably noticed standing way back at the entrance of the outer court of men. And then he self-consciously counts all his accomplishments. First, "I fast twice a week." There was a common time of fasting which everybody was obliged to observe and a private fast which was voluntary and this was generally kept on Mondays and Thursdays. It was this voluntary fast, twice weekly, that the Pharisee was thinking of in his prayer. Then he goes on, "I give tithes of all that I possess." According to Deuteronomy (14:22), except for the tithes on cattle, all products of corn, cider and oil were subject to tithing. Rabbinical interpretation of this law even included vegetables with pods, greens and herbs. As mentioned before, the Pharisees had formed associations to avoid neglecting the slightest duty of tithing. Maybe the Pharisee was thinking of this, but perhaps he meant even more, such as every kind of income and property, all of which he was tithing. In any case he was going far beyond what the law prescribed. Was not everyone, even God, impressed by his high degree of piety?

In the meantime the publican was "standing afar off" in the outer court of men. And he did not even dare lift his eyes to heaven, but with bowed head he strikes his breast as an expression of shame and repentance before God. He does not list a single accomplishment, as the Pharisee has done so well, but only appeals to the mercy of God: "O God, be merciful to me a sinner" (the true sense would be better expressed by saying: ". . .though I am a sinner"). Thus he prays in the words of Psalm 51.

And now Jesus proclaims a surprising verdict, for this publican, who—in the eyes of all those models of piety—is nothing but a scoundrel, this very man, "went down into his house justified rather than the other." With the publican God is able to do something, for behind the passive word "justified" there is concealed, according to an expression of late Judaism, the true subjective, God. God has justified the publican. In God's eyes he is the one who is right and not the Pharisee, though the latter thought himself to be just *and to all appearances is so.* Why? The publican judges himself correctly, repents of his sins, humiliates himself before God and honestly admits that he is a sinner; whereas the Pharisee does not even mention this by one word and does not even realize that he, too, is a poor sinner—as the rest of men. "Instead, he only counts all his accomplishments and, in that illusion about himself, even thanks God that he is not an "unjust" man.

What is consequently the lesson of this parable? If we consider the context in which our parable was fitted into the gospel of St. Luke, it seems that the theme of prayer was what prompted the evangelist to add this parable to the one of the godless judge (see the first ten verses in Chapter 18). Primarily then the question seems to evolve around the kind of disposition, the interior attitude we should assume while praying. The answer is that our attitude should be that of the publican and not that of the Pharisee. But is this really the primary kerygma of our parable? In the parable of the god-less judge it is not the figure of the widow but that of the judge which holds the central position in the story; and correspondingly, God holds this position in the factual part of the parable. It is very similar to the parable of the Pharisee and the publican. Not these two figures, but God holds the central position, for the question is, how does *God* react to the prayers of these men? And what Jesus wishes to proclaim about God in this parable is, that God does not justify him who justifies himself but rather him who repents and is a humble sinner. This of course brings to mind a second lesson which cannot be sep-arated from the foregoing one, namely, that God is mainly interested in what the Bible calls "conver-sion," as exemplified by the publican. He exempli-fied, because the very essence of a conversion is uniquely revealed by the prayer of the publican. Thus it is the decision to *radically change his opin-ion about himself and his past,* the decision to "transform his way of thinking," which is expressed by the Greek word *metanoia.*

     At the end of this parable the evangelist Luke adds another of Jesus' special warnings (see v. 14); it is a verdict, a so-called wandering phrase (*logion*) which also appears elsewhere in St. Luke (14:11) and in St. Matthew (23:12). St. Luke placed Jesus' warning at the close of this parable because he actually wanted to re-emphasize the twofold lesson: God will humble him who exalts himself (that is, at judgment time) and exalt him who humbles himself!

DIVINE AND HUMAN WAYS
OF THINKING

The Prodigal Son
(Luke 15:11–32)

If the interpretation of a parable calls for a special consideration of the details of its story, then this applies particularly to the parable of the prodigal son.

Jesus tells us about a man who had two sons. One day the younger of the two comes to his father and demands his share of the fortune. The father is instantly willing to fulfill the wish of his younger son, and so he "divided unto them his substance." This is already a point which gives us an idea as to what kind of father he is: he lets his son have his way and gives him complete freedom. The son does not hesitate to use this freedom to its fullness. He takes his inherited portion, which probably consists mainly of money, and then he leaves his home to go into "a far country." There he gradually spends his entire fortune by leading a dissolute life till nothing is left of his goods. Chance so has it that a famine breaks out in that country. Perhaps those who listened to this parable for the first time were reminded of the Old Testament story about Joseph's meager years in Egypt. Even our rogue in this parable begins to feel the deprivation to his own body, but what will he do? Should he return home? He does not consider that yet, but he has no money and so there is nothing left to do but hire himself out to one of the big landowners of that country. He becomes a swineherd—something the Jewish listeners of this parable find especially distasteful. And even so, we know that he does not fare well at all because there is so little to eat that "he would fain have filled his belly with the husks" he feeds to the swine. In his dire need he finally reflects upon his own failings and upon the riches and happiness he enjoyed in his father's house, which he had left with so much ingratitude and thoughtlessness. As he starts on his way back, he ponders upon what he will say to his father, since he does not know how he will be received at home.

While he is still a good distance from his father's farm, the father espies him. What does this imply? It means that the father is ever looking out for his son, perhaps from a near hilltop or from the flat roof of his house, which would permit a wide view of the countryside. Perhaps he has gone there daily in the secret hope of seeing his son return one day. And then the father sees him coming and he recognizes him immediately, though he is still far away and greatly changed in appearance. Now his son is clothed in rags. Destitute in body and mind he trudges along wearily, and all the misery of body and soul is written on his face. The father is deeply moved. He hastens to greet his returning son and falls upon his neck, kissing him as a sign of his pardoning love. The son admits his guilt, but the father does not even let him finish his confession. One should notice here that the returning son is not even able to say all the words he intended to address to his father (compare v. 18, 19 with v. 21). Instead, the father orders his servants to "bring forth quickly the first robe, and put it on him, and put a ring on his hand, and shoes on his feet." The young man is promptly reinstated as one of his father's sons! According to the story of this parable, this scene takes place outside, at the point where father and son met again, and consequently the prodigal son *returned to his father's house in his newly won dignity* and thus his former state of misery is not exposed to the public eye. The father wishes to avoid exposing this son of his who has returned full of repentance. And then the fatted calf is killed and a great meal takes place, because this his son "was dead and is come to life again; he was lost, and is found."

This is the end of the first part of the parable. What is the lesson Jesus wishes to teach us? To fully realize it, we must first give thought to the way the father could have treated his returning son. There are three possibilities: first, the father could have driven away his returning son at once, saying: "Go where you belong, to your old pals and girl friends! You have brought nothing but shame upon your whole family, you scoundrel; the whole village is gossiping about us, and we scarcely dare show ourselves"; or, he could have offered his son a time of probation, something the homecomer seemed to have hoped for ("make me as one of thy hired servants"); or, the father could have kept silent without taking any further notice of him, and this might have been the worst punishment for the returning son. But he chose none of these courses! Instead, the father is as happy as a child whose parents return from a long journey. He even showers his returned son with the strongest sign of his love; he reinstates him fully and completely as his son. One might even say that the returned son, who was lost and was found again, is now more loved than before, and that is the incredible point of our parable.

Now, of whom does Jesus really speak? He speaks of God, for it is the father, and not the son, who stands in the center of this story. This is the way God acts towards sinners who find their way back to Him, and are converted, for this is the true sentiment of God. At the same time we realize in a unique manner what the word "conversion" means in its biblical sense; it means a "going home," a "turning back," which definitely corresponds to the Hebrew expression for the Greek word *metanoia*. In this sense the parable of the prodigal son complements that of the Pharisee and the publican. While we understood that "conversion" in the other parable implied a radical change of opinion about oneself, this concept is now complemented by the idea that a conversion is tantamount to a return to the Father.

The parable could now end with the return and acceptance of the son by the father, but Jesus continues His story. "Now his elder son was in the field, and when he came and drew nigh to the house, he heard music and dancing: And he called one of

the servants, and asked what these things meant.
And he said to him: Thy brother is come, and thy
father hath killed the fatted calf, because he hath
received him safe. And he was angry, and would
not go in. His father therefore coming out began to
entreat him. And he answering, said to his father:
Behold, for so many years do I serve thee, and I
have never transgressed thy commandment, and
yet thou hast never given me a kid to make merry
with my friends." One should notice that the older
brother in his anger does not even use the title
"Father" when he addresses him (compare v. 29
with v. 21). Thus he creates a distance between
himself and his father just as he refuses to call his
brother by his title: "But as soon as this thy son is
come, who hath devoured his substance with harlots, thou hast killed for him the fatted calf." Perhaps the fatted calf had been reserved for the older
brother's marriage, but the return of the younger
son is important enough for the father to have the
fatted calf killed. Yet, the father says to him: "Son,"
—notice the affectionate way of addressing him—
"thou art always with me, and all I have is thine
(that is, you can always have a feast with your
friends as often as you like). But it was fit that we
should make merry and be glad, for this thy brother
was dead and is come to life again; he was lost and
is found." This now is the second part of our parable. But why did Jesus add this part at all? He did
so, because He wished to reveal not only God's way
of thinking but, in contrast, the completely different way of men's thinking. Just as the older son

judged the younger one, so also do men judge those
who are sinners, even if they are converted. They
do not rejoice over the return of a sinner as God
does. For them a sinner is something final. They
even protest against the Father's mercy! And this
kind of protest was, according to the gospel, the
true reason for Jesus to tell this parable at all. He
had been reproached for consorting in a friendly
manner with publicans and sinners who had come
to Him, eager for salvation. One needs only to read
the verses which serve as an introduction to the
three parables in St. Luke, that of the lost sheep, the
lost groat, and the prodigal son: "Now the publicans and sinners drew near unto him to hear him.
And the Pharisees and the scribes murmured, saying: This man receiveth sinners and (even) eateth
with them" (15:1, 2). Through the interpretation of
the parable of the Pharisee and the publican we
know that the Pharisee kept himself at a safe distance from the publicans and similar people, who in
his eyes were notorious sinners, for he was meticu-
lously anxious to avoid any communication with
them. Therefore it must have been very annoying
and irritating for the Pharisees to see that Jesus
preferably chose to associate with sinners and announced to them the message of God's kingdom.
Jesus had even drawn one of these "scoundrels,"
the publican Levi, into His intimate circle of disciples and quite freely shared His table with any and
all such sinners (see Mark 2:15–17). And now He
defends His actions and way of thinking by showing
His critics with these three parables that they have

no idea what God is really like: "God is not the way *you* think He is, but the way He is represented in the stories of my parables. Heaven rejoices more over the return of one sinner than over ninety-nine just! That is why I have to act thus towards publicans and all those who, in your eyes, are lost forever, because this is how God acts! And that is why the sermon of Jesus is called a "message of joy" (in Greek *euangelion*).

Jesus never told us the other part of this parable. We do not know what the older brother really did—whether or not he acquiesced with his father's wish, greeting the returned brother and taking part at the merry feast. Jesus probably left this story deliberately open as an appeal to His judges to end their criticism and to be considerate of sinners who crave for salvation, as God is considerate and He also. If His critics are not ready to do so, *then they are the ones who in the end will be lost forever.*

THE GOOD MASTER
OF THE VINEYARD

The Laborers of the Vineyard
(Matt. 20:1–16)

At certain times of the year there is much work to be done in a vineyard. This is well known among the unemployed day laborers and so, early in the morning, they go to the market place where the winegrowers congregate to hire laborers for their vineyards. And now Jesus tells us in the story of His parable about such a winegrower, a "householder," who goes out quite early in the morning to the market place, to hire day laborers for the work in his vineyard. He briefly discusses wages with some of them and soon they agree upon a penny, the minimum pay for a day. Those who are hired go immediately to the vineyard and begin their work. We are not told if it is vintage time, but the laborers are obviously familiar with this kind of work and do not need any further instructions.

When the master returns to the market place a few hours later, "around the third hour," that is, between eight and nine o'clock in the morning, he sees other men standing around who are also willing to work but who have not as yet been hired. He therefore sends them out to his vineyard without settling the exact amount of pay, saying: "I will give you what shall be just." Of course, this is said deliberately by Jesus with regard to the outcome of the story. The master of the vineyard seems to know exactly what he wants in the end, and so, later on, when he goes back to the market place several times and still finds unhired laborers, he also sends them to his vineyard. Even an hour before evening ("about the eleventh hour") all this is again repeated. Jesus does not tell us this to explain that the winegrower needs more laborers than he had counted on in the morning; rather He wants to emphasize even in this part of His story how very kind the householder was toward those poor, unemployed day laborers, for he is a good master who is willing to let them all earn something.

When evening comes, Jesus continues, the master of the vineyard orders his steward to pay the day laborers their wages. Strangely enough, the steward begins—surely with the knowledge of his master—to first pay those who had come at the eleventh hour to work in the vineyard. And behold, they receive a full penny though they had only worked for one hour. The others see this, especially those who had been in the vineyard since early morning, and so expect a higher pay than that agreed upon. However, they too receive but the one penny for which they had settled. At this point of the story the parable could easily end, for a very important lesson about the kingdom of God has already become evident. This is a parable treating of the kingdom of God which signifies that God in His mercy even rewards those who do not deserve it. But, as in other parables, Jesus deliberately continues with the story: the day laborers who had worked all day in the vineyard without receiving more than those who were hired last begin to "murmur" against the master of the house (v. 11). They voice their indignation by saying: "These last have worked *but* one hour, and thou hast made them equal to us," though we have labored all day long and suffered the heat at noon, whereas the others have only worked one hour in the cool evening. Is that just?

The winegrower replies to the loudest among them: "Friend, I do thee no wrong: didst thou not agree with me for a penny? Take what is thine and go thy way: I will also give to this last even as to thee. Or, is it not lawful for me to do what I will? Is thy eye evil, because I am good?" (v. 13–15). This is his answer, but does the proprietor of a vineyard normally act this way? Certainly not, because such magnanimity and conduct of business would soon lead to his ruin. Yet, in spite of this fact, the winegrower in this story told by Jesus acts in this improbable manner and Jesus tells us this because He wishes to give us a message about the kingdom of God. We realized earlier that in this parable God Himself is represented by the owner of the vineyard. But what about those who "murmured"; who are they? It seems obvious that the evangelist did not transmit the original situation of our parable but brought it into a new context, for we also find those who murmur in St. Luke (15:2)—but there it refers to the Pharisees and the scribes—and again men who murmur against Jesus Himself because

He accepts the publicans and the sinners (19:7). There is much ill will against Jesus among the Pharisees and scribes because He is kind to sinners, and it was against these murmurers that our parable seems to have been primarily directed. What Jesus really wanted to tell these people with His parable was: "You do not know anything about the reign of God! God is not the way you imagine Him to be, for God is not the representative of a legal point as you are. Rather, God is merciful, as merciful and kind as only Love can be." This is the essential lesson which Jesus wants to impart with His parable. He shows us God's sentiment, His way of thinking. Thus we have, in the center of the parable, the winegrower and not the laborers. At the same time, this parable is also meant to bring out the sentiment of men whose thoughts are narrow and obstinate and who cannot rejoice that God is even merciful to those who do not fully deserve it. With their murmuring men reveal their criticism of God, and that is why there is a continuation of the parable's story. It implies: This is the way God is, and this is the way you are!—which is the lesson of our parable.

The context in which this parable is placed in the gospel of St. Matthew serves as a justification of the promise made by Jesus to the Apostles; that it is they who will sit on twelve thrones to judge the twelve tribes of Israel at the Last Judgment and not those who, to all appearance, are the first among their people (see 19:28, 30). The last verse, "And many that are first, shall be last: and the last shall be first" (19:30), is indeed a summary which brings out clearly that this is the main lesson of our parable in its *context with the gospel*. It remains an astounding fact, after all, that these unknown and uneducated fishermen and peasants of Galilee (and not the Prophets) will one day judge the people of Israel. This calls for a justification, and in response, our parable gives us God's free and great mercy as the final reason.

CONSTANT READINESS
FOR DEATH

The Foolish Farmer
(Luke 12:16–21)

According to the message of the gospel, Jesus had a special reason for telling us this parable (see 12:13–15). Some man from the crowd approaches Jesus and asks Him to intervene in a misunderstanding over an inheritance. Jesus sharply refuses to do so: "Man, who hath appointed me judge (in this village), or divider, over you?" In this dispute brought to His attention, Jesus clearly recognizes human covetousness again at work, and that the unfortunate "wish-for-more" (the exact expression for the Greek word meaning covetousness) is the main drive in this matter. That is why Jesus warns us immediately and urgently by saying: "Take heed, and beware of all covetousness; for a man's (real) life doth not consist in the abundance of things which he possesseth" (v. 15). To unmask the shortsightedness and folly revealed by acts of covetousness, Jesus tells us the following parable (v. 16–20):

In a certain year, the land of a wealthy farmer unexpectedly brings forth an abundance of fruit. His barns are much too small to store this great blessing of produce from his fields. For a

while the farmer thinks about what he should do to
store his harvest properly, and then he has an idea
(a very natural one at that): "I will pull down my
barns, and will build greater; and into them will I
gather all things that are grown to me, and my
goods." Now, there is nothing wrong with this, for
many farmers will do the same if they want to be
good business men. But in this story the farmer is
moved by an unusual thought: "And I will say to
my soul: Soul, thou hast much goods laid up for
many years, take thy rest; eat, drink, make good
cheer." Thus, the farmer does not intend to go on
working in the years to come but wants to enjoy
a comfortable and luxurious life by using up his
stored provisions, He gives no thought to the distant
future, not even to his real future—his true existence. That God may have other plans for him does
not occur to him at all; however, God intends to call
him from this life: "But God said to him: Thou fool,
this night do they require thy soul of thee: and
whose shall those things be which thou hast provided?" This farmer is indeed a fool because he
thinks only of his earthly life and not of his fate in
eternity. He does not consider, in his foolishness,
that he cannot really dispose of his own life the way
he imagined he could because another One is the
Lord of his life. Of all his riches there is nothing he
will be able to take with him to eternity. He will
have to leave everything to his heirs. How will he
fare at judgment time? This is a question which
Jesus neither asks nor answers, but it looms distinctly in the background of His parable. For what

He really wants to say is: "Forget about that (unfortunate) 'wish-for-more!' Instead, concern yourself about being ready at all times to appear before
the judgment seat of God. Give thought to the last
things and assure yourself an 'eschatological' existence, your true life! He who is only concerned about
his earthly life instead of becoming 'rich towards
God' is a fool like the farmer in my parable" (v. 21).

One is inclined to call this parable of the
foolish farmer a "parable of crisis" which Jesus
told in the face of the threatening catastrophe, but
verse 20 brings out clearly that the disaster which
is coming upon the wealthy farmer is not that of the
final catastrophe—the end of the world—but the individual catastrophe of a sudden death. The death of
this man is a catastrophe because, in his foolishness and shortsightedness, he thinks only of his
earthly life and his bourgeois comfort rather than
of God and the ultimate things. (Here see also the
words of Jesus in St. Luke (9:25): "For what is a
man advantaged of, if he gain the whole world, and
lose himself, and cast away himself?"). Besides,
there is no doubt that for the story of His parable
Jesus uses a wise pronouncement taken from the
Old Testament, from the Book of Sirach (Eccl.
11:18 f.):

There is one that is enriched by living sparingly,
and this is the portion of his reward. In that he
saith: I have found me rest, and now I will eat of
my goods alone: And he knoweth not what time
shall pass, and that death approacheth, and that
he must leave all to others, and shall die.

This is a very clear indication of earthly death. And this is what Jesus reminds us of in the parable of the foolish farmer.

A CONVERSION IN
GOOD TIME

The Rich Man and Poor Lazarus
(Luke 16:19–31)

The man of whom Jesus speaks in this parable is "rich," and in the Orient this means that his status is one of influence and importance. He clothes himself in purple (according to I Machabee 8:14, the robe of a king is purple) and in linen, both regarded as great luxuries—for the simple people wear garments of wool. This man lives riotously and in splendor, and daily gives sumptuous feasts of the choicest food and finest wines for his friends and brothers. This glutton lives very much like the godless men in the Book of Wisdom (2:6–9), who say: "Come, therefore, and let us enjoy the good things that are present, and let us speedily use the creatures as in youth. Let us fill ourselves with costly wine, and ointments: and let not the flower of the time pass by us. Let us crown ourselves with roses, before they be withered: let no meadow escape our riot. Let none of us go without his part in luxury: let us everywhere leave tokens of our joy: for this is our portion, and this *our* lot." In the meantime, there lies a poor man at the entrance gate of the rich man's palace. According to the Greek text, he had been "put down" there. He is so

miserable and weak that he can no longer walk by
himself, and so his poor relatives bring him daily to
the gate of the rich man's palace where elegant
gentlemen go in and out. There he is supposed to
beg so as to sustain himself a little longer. He must
have made a pitiful impression on those who passed
by; Jesus tells us that his body is "full of sores,"
blood and pus trickling down from them. Evidently
he is clothed only in a few rags which scarcely
cover his nakedness. Inside the palace, the feast is
proceeding, and the fat drips off the hands of the
diners. As is the custom, thin slices of bread are
used to wipe the hands and are then dropped on the
floor. Poor Lazarus would have been glad to have
this bread, but nobody cares about him. Laughing
and intoxicated, the friends of the rich man pass
him by, and the glances they cast at him are full of
contempt and arrogance. Wild dogs, which roam
the Orient, coming to lick his wounds, seem to have
more compassion on this poor fellow than these
men who do not bother about his festering wounds.
No wonder that death soon overcomes poor Lazarus, which for him is a deliverance. But now his
fate changes abruptly, for angels carry him up to
the heavenly banquet, where he is given a place of
honor at the right side of Abraham—and that is
what is meant by being taken up into Abraham's
bosom.

But for the rich man too, one day, the last
hour comes—even sooner than expected, because
he has lived so sumptuously. Though he is buried
with great pomp by his friends and fellow citizens

("first class!") he must nevertheless descend into hell where he suffers torments for his godless life and behavior on earth. As he lifts his eyes toward heaven he sees afar the Patriarch Abraham and, lying in his bosom, Lazarus. According to a perception of Late Judaism, the condemned are able to see the joy of the blessed so as to increase their own agony. The rich man immediately recognizes Lazarus, a sign that he had often noticed him lying there at the entrance of his palace, though he never gave any thought to the thirst and needs of this poor man. Now the rich man would be happy if he had only one drop of water from the river flowing in Paradise (see Apoc. 22:1 f.), for he says: "I am tormented in this flame." But Abraham is not able to fulfill his wish because "between us and you (between heaven and hell), there is fixed a great chaos," which no man can pass. The glutton's destiny to be in hell is unalterable and, besides that, Abraham draws his attention to the compensating justice which has now become effective in the different ends known in the other world by these two deceased men. Now, both possess what they deserve: the poor man, eternal consolation; and the rich man, eternal torment—thus, times have changed!

This is where the story could end. One lesson —that of *God's compensating justice*—is quite obvious. But Jesus continues with v. 27 ff. The rich man begs Abraham to send Lazarus into the house of his father to warn his brothers that a similar fate awaits them who are still merrily continuing their riotous life. But this plea, too, is denied by Abra-

ham, who points out that: "They have Moses and
the prophets," that is, Holy Scripture. They have
enough opportunities to become acquainted with
God's will and His warnings; "let them hear them"
and be converted! But the condemned man is not
content with this for apparently nothing that he had
read in Holy Scripture had had any effect on him
while he was still on earth. He knows his five
brothers will also be heedless of this warning, but
he believes that he has found a better solution
to bring about their conversion and so he says:
". . .but if one went to them from the dead, they
will do penance." If poor Lazarus, whom they had
all known, were to appear to them suddenly from
eternity, then indeed this would make a deep impression on them—a bourgeois opinion which is
widespread! Abraham does not share this idea for:
"If they hear not Moses and the prophets, neither
will they believe, if one rise again from the dead."
He who does not care about God's will as revealed
in Holy Scripture will not change, even if he wit-
nesses the greatest miracle. Whoever thinks he
would deludes himself. The unbelieving world
would only offer some kind of wise explanation or
cheap excuse, rather than be converted, just as the
religious leaders of the Jews failed to be converted
when Jesus raised Lazarus of Bethany from the
dead. On the contrary, the gospel tells us that the
high priests resolved "to kill Lazarus also, because
many of the Jews, by reason of him, went away,
and believed in Jesus" (John 12:10 f.).

These thoughts of the rich man at the end of

the story, concerning the conversion of his still-living brothers, prove that he himself had been without repentance during his life. Perhaps he had not even been godless. Perhaps he had attended the divine service regularly, where he had listened to the words of Holy Scripture, to God's warnings and encouragement to be converted; but, engulfed by his life of gluttony, he had not drawn the right conclusions—until it was too late.

What is it that Jesus wishes to teach us in this parable? What is its salient point? It is seen in Christ's rejection of the Pharisee's belief in retaliation, by which wealth and poverty were regarded as expressions of divine favor or punishment. However, the Pharisees likewise would have abhorred the rich man's way of life, because the giving of alms, a demand of Scripture, topped the list of their moral code. Another viewpoint of the main theme of this parable could be the rejection of signs from Jesus (see Luke 11:29–32), or a warning about wealth (Luke 18:24): "How hardly shall they that have riches enter into the kingdom of God. For it is easier for a camel to pass through the eye of a needle, than for a rich man to enter into the kingdom of God." In other words, it is the lesson Jesus taught about God's compensating justice (in the first part of the parable). All these ideas are correct and can be gathered from this parable but, nevertheless, the essential lesson seems to be that which is stressed in the second part of the story. It is that quality which the rich man lacked completely, namely, the *will to be converted,* though he was familiar with God's demands and warnings from Holy Scripture. But he did not take these warnings seriously and instead probably cherished the opinion that after death everything would be over, anyway; therefore he would resolve to live now in ease and comfort! A conversion is quite uncalled for, and as for the poor, let them starve for that is their fate (Wisd. 2:1–5).

Thus Jesus seems to have used this parable mostly to warn the rich: *"Be converted in time, before it is too late;* lest your fate be that of the rich glutton in the story of my parable."* In this case, the man's will to be converted could have found expression by using his unjust mammon to win friends among the poor (Luke 16:9).

It would be quite wrong to draw too many dogmatic conclusions from our parable—for example, according to what Jesus said, that there might possibly exist after all a relationship between the blessed in heaven and the damned; or, that Jesus rejected the doctrine of Purgatory with this parable; and so on. What concerns the story of this parable is that Jesus fully conforms with the views of Late Judaism and uses them to gain the attention of His listeners. And precisely this fact, which takes the eschatology of Late Judaism into account, attests to the reliable transmission of this parable.

LAST TIME OF GRACE
FOR ISRAEL

The Barren Fig Tree
(Luke 13:6–9)

"Someone" is the owner of a vineyard and besides the vine he has also planted fruit trees, among them a fig tree. This is quite a choice place for a fig tree to grow because, normally, it would have to content itself with far poorer soil and really does not need any special attention. Now this fig tree in the vineyard has grown to the point where it could normally be expected to bear fruit, but it is in vain that the master of the vineyard looks for them. This master is extraordinarily patient, for only after another two or three years, in which the fig tree does not bear any fruit, does he finally decide to have it uprooted because of its barrenness. The gardener, however, puts in a good word for the tree: "Lord, let it alone this year also, until I dig about it and dung it. And if happily it bear fruit: but if not, then after that thou shalt cut it down." Apparently the owner of the vineyard gives in to this plea, but Jesus does not tell whether this time of grace actually helped the tree to bear fruit in the following year. Of course, Jesus deliberately withheld this knowledge because His parable is meant to en-

courage fruits of penance. *Who*, then, is to bring
forth this fruit?

We know nothing about the occasion which
primarily induced Jesus to tell this parable, since
its present place in the gospel was probably determined by the evangelist. The latter, though, makes
it clear that Israel is what He meant by the fig tree
and that it is to Israel that God granted a last
period of grace (see also Osee 9:10; Mic. 7:1; Jer.
8:13)—to Israel, which is called upon with a threatening warning of the coming judgment to make use
of this period and bring forth true "fruits" of penance. The introductory words of warning (Luke
13:3–5) are expressly directed to Israel, to the Galileans and the citizens of Jerusalem, who are told:
". . . unless you shall do penance, you shall all likewise perish" (like the Galileans murdered by Pilate
and the eighteen men of Jerusalem who were killed
by a falling tower). And this time of grace, granted
to Israel by God, is not just any phase of its history
but the one in which the Messias, Jesus, is actively
dwelling in their midst, calling them to penance, to
conversion (see 13:5: "Beware ye of the signs of the
time!") though Jesus cannot be identified allegorically with the gardener in the parable's story.

Thus it seems that this parable of Jesus was
told before the decision was definitely taken against
Him which, later on, brought about the great judgment over Israel (Luke 13:34; 14:24; 19:41–44;
20:16–18; 21:5 f.).

The permanent lesson of this parable implies: God is infinitely patient, but there comes a time when even the last period of grace granted by Him finally ends and then there remains nothing but judgment!

THE UNHEEDED HOUR
OF GOD

Moody Children
(Matt. 11:16 f.; Luke 7:31 f.)

"But whereunto shall I esteem this generation to be like? It is like to children sitting in the
marketplace. Who crying to their companions say:
We have piped to you, and you have not danced;
we have lamented, and you have not mourned."

According to the form in which St. Matthew
handed this text down to us, we must imagine the
scene to be as follows: children, perhaps boys and
girls, wish to play at weddings and funerals. To
this purpose they divide into two groups in the
marketplace. The one group is supposed to represent the musicians, the other one the dancers or the
mourners. But alas, when either the piping of the
flutes or the lamentations begin, the second group
neither wants to dance nor strike their breasts; and
so the planned games are not performed at all, for
the children belonging to the second group had lost
their interest before the playing began, the way
children often do when they are at play. They are
moody, obstinate and self-willed; and so a fight
starts between the two groups, and they give up
playing and just sit around in the marketplace. The
musicians reproach those who were in the group of

the dancers: "We have piped to you and you have not danced; we have lamented, and you have not mourned."

St. Luke gives us a somewhat different version of the text: while the one group pipes the marriage songs on their flutes, the others are supposed to dance, but these do not want it this way and, instead, begin on their own with the lamentations, whereupon the first group refuses to strike their breasts. And so they reproach each other, after they all sit down again in the marketplace.

This is a very simple parable drawn from experience with children, but what does Jesus wish to tell us? He compares, as He says in His introduction, "this generation" to children, or to be quite exact, to their behavior. Why? To understand this, one should consider the context in which these verses are fitted into the parable, because Jesus immediately gives us the reason why He compares "this generation" to moody children with the following: "For John came neither eating nor drinking; and they say: He hath a devil. The son of man came eating and drinking, and they say: Behold a man that is a glutton and a wine drinker, a friend of the publicans and sinners." Thus, the adversaries of the Baptist regard his stern asceticism as a kind of insanity, a demoniac possession. Their hasty and critical judgment decides that he could have led such an austere life only with the aid of a demon. And this is all they have to say about him. Later on, they see that Jesus seems to enjoy meals, which He frequently shares with people who, in the eyes of these models of piety, are lost forever; and so they reproach Him for being a glutton and a wine drinker, a friend of the publicans and sinners.

From the gospels we know that Jesus actually did take part at some meals in the company of "publicans and sinners," something the scribes and the Pharisees held very much against Him (see Mark 2:15 f.; Luke 15:1 f.; and also the parable of the prodigal son). They are angered about His conduct and sentiment and completely misjudge the real intention which prompted Jesus to share the table of publicans and sinners. By acting thus, Jesus wanted to tell these poor people that in the eyes of *God* they are never lost as long as they are sincerely willing to be converted (as was the publican in the Temple). In behaving towards them in this way, Jesus reveals God's true sentiment, His forgiving kindness and mercy. Moreover, by freely eating with publicans and sinners Jesus wants to stress, in connection with His other Messianic works, that *now the Messianic time of salvation has begun—*"Be ye aware of this!" His enemies, however, are incapable of recognizing the hour, the *kairos* (crosspoint), the working of God. They remain blind in the face of what is happening before their very eyes, and they pronounce judgments which only show that they resemble moody children who refuse to go along when the game is about to begin. The adversaries of Jesus refuse to open their hearts and to thank and praise God that the promised and longed-for Messias has finally come to dwell among them. They acted in very much the same way toward the Baptist. His call to penance was also rejected by them in contrast to the publican's reaction, and they refused to be baptized by St. John whose severe life of penance was interpreted by them as a kind of demoniac possession, not realizing that this was meant to be a preparation for the One Who was to come (Luke 7:29).

Thus, the adversaries of Jesus—"this generation"— do not recognize the hour of God. They remain blind, though they maintain they are those "who see" (John 9:39–41), and therefore Jesus compares them to moody children who do not know what they want.

The enduring lesson imparted by this parable is: Do not become hardened, but heed the hour, the call and the will of God! Be ye aware of the signs of the time!

AGAINST THE FALSE
SHEPHERDS OF ISRAEL

The Wicked Tenants of the Vineyard
(Mark 12:1–11; Matt. 21:33–44; Luke 20:9–18)

"A *certain* man"—Jesus does not say who it is—"planted a vineyard and made a hedge about it, and dug a place for the winevat and built a tower. . . ." With these words of the Prophet Isaias (see Isa. 5:1 f.) Jesus begins this parable. The building of a vineyard on the stony slopes of Palestine is very hard work, but now it is finished, and soon exquisite fruit can be expected to grow forth. Because of some pressing business, the master of the vineyard has to leave for a long journey which may even take him to a foreign country, and so he leases his vineyard to small farmers. The owner is an expert in his field and knows exactly when the vineyard will bear fruit for the first time; so he sends a servant, one of his stewards, to the tenants to collect the rent. These tenants, however, act in a very strange manner. They refuse to be reminded of the contract and are quite indignant when the steward of their landlord comes to them. Their indignation even goes so far that they beat the steward and send him back to the landlord. The master of the vineyard, on the other hand, shows a degree of patience which is quite unbelievable, for he sends an-

other servant to his tenants but also this one is
ill-treated and insulted by them. Then a third servant is sent—what incredible patience!—"and him
they killed." Not even now does the master of the
vineyard intervene personally but goes on sending
"many others" with the same result, for they also
are either beaten or killed by the tenants. Nobody
in the whole world would take a thing like that except the master of the vineyard in the parable of
Jesus. And though the story of this parable sounds
unbelievable enough up to now, Jesus goes on to tell
us the following about the owner of the vineyard:
"Therefore having yet one son, most dear to him;
he also sent him unto them last of all, saying: They
will reverence my son" (v. 6). But he is mistaken,
for the arrival of the son does not bring the tenants
to their senses; on the contrary, they see this only
as a unique opportunity to acquire the whole vineyard for themselves: "This is the heir; come let us
kill him; and the inheritance shall be ours!" And
they take hold of the son, kill him, and throw his
body out of the vineyard.

At this point of the story, Jesus interrupts
His narration and asks His audience (which, according to Mark 11:27, consists of some well-known
Jewish theologians and spiritual authorities—"the
chief priests and the scribes and the ancients"),
surely listening to Him with great interest, the following question: "What therefore will the lord of
the vineyard do?" According to St. Mark and St.
Luke, however, Jesus immediately answers this
question Himself: "He will come and destroy *those*

husbandmen; and will give the vineyard to others." With this reply the story of the parable has reached its conclusive high point. The subsequent text (Ps. 118:22 f.) which Jesus quotes in a menacing tone before His aforementioned audience (Mark 12:10 f.), was perhaps primarily cited by Him in another context, but it fits perfectly into this passage because it serves to clarify who the son in the parable's story is really meant to be: it is the *Messias* Whom the builders rejected but Whom God had designated to be the cornerstone of His new building (see also Apoc. 4:11; I Pet. 2:6–8). Then we gather from the following sentences of the gospel what impression this parable made upon the listeners of Jesus: "And they sought to lay hands on him, but they feared the people. For they knew that he spoke this parable to them." This then shows us clearly what Jesus wished to tell His audience: "This is the way you are, you high priests, scribes and ancients, for you take the same attitude towards the messengers of God, even towards His Son, as the tenants in the story of my parable. And not only are you thus, but the spiritual leaders of Isreal have always behaved like this." The "vineyard," quoted by Jesus at the beginning of the parable, is Israel, planted by God Himself (see Isa. 5:1 f.), and the tenants are the spiritual leaders of God's people in the Old Testament. The various servants, which the owner sends into his vineyard to collect the fruits belonging to him, are the Prophets of the Old Covenant, and from what the Old Testament tells us, they were often received most ungraciously and full of contempt, and their admonitions and warnings were always left unheeded (see also Matt. 23:29–39). "Last of all" God sends His Son, the Heir of the vineyard, but He also suffers the same fate as the Prophets: He is killed and cast away.

It is the concrete history of salvation which looms behind the story of this parable, and that is why it sounds so utterly strange and improbable, especially concerning the behavior of the vineyard's proprietor. God is infinitely patient and forebearing, but sometimes even His patience comes to an end. The murdering of His Son leads to a severe punishment and rejection of Israel's leaders by God. The tenants are killed—the destruction of Jerusalem in the year 70—and the vineyard is "given to others," to the "servants" of Jesus, the Apostles, for He probably had them in mind. Thus the parable of the wicked tenants is directed as a threat *against the false shepherds of Israel*. The allusions to the history of salvation contained in this parable are no added "allegorizations," else a new vineyard would certainly have been mentioned; rather these allusions already existed in the original composition. However, they may have been clarified to a certain extent by the evangelists, especially by St. Matthew and St. Luke, in the light of the Christian faith.

THE ACCOUNTING

Entrusted Money
(Matt. 25:14–30; Luke 19:12–27)

The form of this parable, handed down to us by St. Matthew, differs considerably from the one we have in St. Luke. Opinions are divergent as to which of them does more justice to the original text. As the parable in St. Luke maintains a much closer connection with profane reality than does St. Matthew's, and because its story seems to make allusions to quite definite events in the history of the Jewish nation, one may judge his text, as is the case in many other instances, as being closer to the original composition. We will therefore give more attention to the story of the parable in St. Luke.

Jesus tells us of a "certain nobleman" who, after going into a far country to receive the dignity of kingship, returns to his own kingdom. Before he departs he summons ten of his servants and gives them ten pounds with the order to trade with this amount until he returns. "But his citizens hated him . . . saying: We will not have this man to reign over us." This they say in vain, for after some time the lord returns as a king. First he demands a strict accounting of what each man has gained with the money entrusted to him and then he holds a devas-

tating judgment over his enemies: ". . . those my
enemies, who would not have me reign over them,
bring them hither, and kill them before me" (v. 27).

This is essentially the story which Jesus, according to the tradition of St. Luke, gives us, and
perhaps He even alludes to certain events of the
year B.C., with which His listeners may have been
familiar. For the Jewish historian Josephus Flavius tells us that Archelaos, the son and testamen-
tal heir of Herod the Great, went to Rome to the
emperor to be acknowledged by him as the new
king in his father's kingdom (see v. 12). While he
was in Rome the Jews sent to the emperor an em-
bassy of about fifty men who complained about
Archelaos and refused to have him as their king
(here see v. 14). Thereupon, Archelaos only became
ethnarch (that is, "regent" of provinces) of the
provinces of Judea, Samaria and Idumea, but not
king of all Palestine. After Archelaos returned to
Jerusalem he immediately dismissed the high priest
Joazar who had sided with his enemies. Then
he cruelly punished the Jews and Samaritans "in
memory of recent conflicts," as Josephus writes
(see v. 27). Yet, the story told by Jesus differs greatly
from Josephus' report. In the parable's story the
lord really returns as a king (v. 15), but as to who
confirmed him remains unsaid. Besides, in the parable by Jesus the passage about the pounds was inserted, and the detailed description of the king's
request for an accounting, after his return, shows
us in verses 15–26 how important this idea was in
the eyes of Jesus. Apparently He had a specific king

in mind, and the story about Archelaos only served as a background setting for the parable and nothing more.

Furthermore, the lesson of this parable is only clear if its middle part, the incident about the entrusted pounds, is given more attention. Before the nobleman goes to receive his kingship he entrusts ten of his servants with ten pounds, "and said to them: Trade till I come." After his return he asks his servants for an accounting. "And the first came, saying: Lord, thy pound hath gained ten pounds. And he said to him: Well done, thou good servant, because thou hast been faithful in a little, thou shalt have power over ten cities. And the second came, saying: Lord, thy pound hath gained five pounds. And he said to him: Be thou also over five cities. And another came saying: Lord, behold here is thy pound, which I have kept laid up in a napkin; for I feared thee, because thou art an austere man: thou takest what thou didst not lay down, and thou reapest that which thou didst not sow. He saith to him: Out of thy own mouth I judge thee, thou wicked servant. Thou knewest that I was an austere man, taking up what I laid down and reaping that which I did not sow: And why then didst thou not give my money into the bank, that at my coming I might exact it with usury?" (Luke 19:16–23).

There is no word about the remaining seven servants, for Jesus has achieved what He wanted to teach us through this parable. The lesson thus implies: *Trade profitably with what God has entrusted to you, because one day you will have to give an*

accounting to Him. Yet, concealed behind the profane circumstances described in this parable there
is a distinct Christological appeal—the nobleman
who returns as a king is evidently Jesus Himself
Who, as king of the Parousia, will demand an accounting from His "servants" and will judge His
enemies sternly (see also Luke 11:29–32; 12:46;
13:27 f; 14:34 f.). Of course, in this description, we
may not automatically transfer all features of this
image of the mighty king to Jesus. Some of them
simply belong to the profane part of the story de-
scribing the details of the parable.

Verses 25 and 26 ("And they said to him:
Lord, he hath ten pounds. But I say to you that
everyone that hath shall be given, and he shall
abound: and from him that hath not, even that
which he hath, shall be taken from him.") seem to
have fitted into the original context by St. Luke,
whereby verse 25 was most likely a personal formulation by this evangelist, for verse 26 can previously
be found in St. Luke (8:18) and correspondingly
in St. Mark (4:25) and in St. Matthew (13:12).
Probably this was primarily a very distinct warning given by Jesus, which could be aptly applied as
a verdict in the parable of the pounds. The nobleman's actions in this parable are comparable to
God's actions when considering judgment. Now,
especially, because of its framework, this parable
written by St. Luke attests to the fact that it belongs
in a certain way to those parables treating of the
kingdom of God. Jesus, according to St. Luke, told
this parable near Jerusalem, and that is why those

who accompanied Him "thought that the kingdom of God should immediately be manifested." But this premature enthusiasm is discouraged by Jesus through the narration of this parable of the entrusted pounds. It signifies that the kingdom of God cannot be manifested *immediately,* as anticipated by all. There must first be a time of probation, and only then will there be the fulfillment of the kingdom of God, inaugurated by the king who will demand a strict accounting.

The context of this parable with the situation shown in the eleventh verse seems to have been rightly established by the evangelist Luke, but its clarifying message relevant to the question of expectation is rooted in the parable itself, for according to its content, an accounting can only take place after a certain time of probation has been given to the servants and after the nobleman returns as king. This shows that the evangelist in composing the parable interpreted its true sense quite correctly. As a result he was able to lessen that aspect of "immediacy" so prevalent in the early Church and thus bring it into the right perspective. Nevertheless, St. Luke made very few changes in the story of this parable. St. Matthew, however, freed this parable of all its historical allusions. The pounds in question were changed to talents which contributed greatly to the added responsibility of the servants, or rather irresponsibility of the lazy ones, thus making the parable's story more credible. In St. Matthew there is no further mention of the judge's enemies, because the parable addresses itself pri-

marily to the Church, according to the general tendency of the gospel of St. Matthew. Yet, even this
parable in St. Matthew, as the context in which it
was written proves, belongs to those which treat of
the Parousia, for the returning nobleman is Christ
Who will be the judge in His Church.

A WARNING OF THE
CLOSED DOOR

The Ten Virgins
(Matt. 25:1–13)

A marriage is to take place with all the usual customs and habits still in use, even today, in some parts of the Orient. As yet the bride is at the house of her parents and there she waits, together with her friends, the bridesmaids, for the coming of the bridegroom. As soon as the arrival of the groom is announced, the bridesmaids go out to meet him—but without the bride—and then they accompany him to the house of the bride. After that, they all proceed to the house of the bridegroom where the marriage feast is to be celebrated.

In this story Jesus tells us nothing about the bride but only about the bridesmaids. That the number of these is ten has nothing to do with the lesson contained in this parable. Five of the virgins, Jesus tells us, are foolish, and five are wise. The foolishness of the five virgins lies in the fact that, though they brought their little lamps along to guide and light the way of the groom and the whole wedding party on its way to the banquet hall, they did not provide for sufficient oil in their little jugs. In line with what the Orient regards to be good manners, the protocol at a celebration like this is not bound

to any time limit, and so it happens that the bridegroom remains quite a while in the house of his parents among his relatives and friends, and thus the
virgins at the house of the bride gradually begin to
grow drowsy, and finally they fall asleep. "And at
midnight there was a cry made: Behold the bridegroom cometh, go ye forth to meet him." Everybody arises and they all begin to retrim their lamps.
It is only now that the foolish virgins notice that
their lamps, because of the prolonged absence of
the groom, are nearly burnt out and that they lack
sufficient provisions of oil. In their embarrassment
they turn to the wise virgins and beg them to give
them some of their oil. But, "the wise answered,
saying: Lest perhaps there be not enough for us and
for you, go ye rather to them that sell, and buy for
yourselves." They do not say this because they are
selfish, but because they are obviously not expect-
ing the rigorous severity which the bridegroom will
manifest later. The foolish virgins accept the well-
meant advice of the wise ones and quickly run to
the merchants to buy some oil, as business life in
the Orient is prolonged far into the night. In the
meantime the bridegroom arrives, "and they that
were ready went in with him to the marriage, and
the door was shut." At this point, however, the story
of the parable takes a turn, which, seen from the
profane side, seems rather improbable. When a
marriage feast takes place, especially in the Orient,
the door is never closed; instead, there is a constant flow of guests which sometimes lasts as long
as seven days. But in the story of this marriage,

told by Jesus, everything is suddenly quite different.
In this case the door is firmly closed after the wedding party enters the banquet hall. Even after the
foolish virgins arrive with fresh oil in their little
lamps and knock at the closed door of the banquet
hall, saying: "Lord, Lord open to us!" this door
remains shut. To their consternation the bridegroom from within answers: "Amen I say to you, I
know you not!" And so the door remains closed and
the bridesmaids who came too late are not admitted
to the marriage feast. No pleading or calling is of
any avail—a final decision has been made.

Thus the story of our parable in its final part
takes a strange and most unexpected turn. The
bridegroom in this story does not behave as a
groom normally would, so it is quite obvious that
Jesus speaks of a very special one and of a special
marriage where other than usual rules are observed. Thus the purpose of this parable serves to
illumine a religious and historical truth of salvation for, according to its introductory verse (25:1),
it is a parable of the kingdom of God, as evidenced
by the ensuing sentence: "Then shall the kingdom
of heaven be like"—the story which follows. With
St. Matthew (7:23), it is Jesus Himself Who "on
that day" answered the "Lord, Lord" sayers with "I
never knew you" (see also Luke 13:25–27). With
the expression "that day," the Day of the Parousia,
the Last Judgment is meant. The Bridegroom's
saying "I know you not" is a verdict, and the
Bridegroom is the returning Lord Himself. Only
those who are "ready" (Matt. 25:10) will be admit-

ted to the feast in the kingdom of God, but no others. The reason for this unexpected and improbable turn in the parable's story, seen from the profane viewpoint, lies therefore in the fact that Jesus speaks descriptively of His Parousia and the Last Judgment and so invites His listeners to be ready at all times because the hour of His coming is uncertain and the danger exists, if there is no due preparation, of arriving in front of a closed door. *Think ye about this—for the door leading to the banquet hall of God's kingdom will one day be irrevocably closed!* This is the essential lesson of the parable and, as a result of this warning, we are urgently reminded to be constantly ready, lest in the end the same fate await us as that of the five foolish virgins. To reach this paraenetical (applicable) goal, the Bridegroom in the story of this parable *has to tarry* (v. 5). This is the fact which actually provides the reason for an invitation to constant preparedness and, therefore, this point could never have been added later on in the posteasterly rendition of this parable's story, just for the sake of encouraging the Christians to prepare for the so-soon-expected but not-appearing Parousia of the Lord. Rather, this message intimated that we should be prepared at all times, so as not to stand before a closed door in the end. This is what Jesus wishes to tell us essentially with this parable, and thus one cannot fail to see its Christological appeal.

THE SOWER WILL RETURN

The Seed Which Grows by Itself
(Mark 4:26–29)

This parable belongs to the so-called parables on growth, which were apparently directed against erroneous ideas about the kingdom of God, widespread among the enemies and even followers of Jesus. The parables of the sower, the cockle and the wheat, the fish net and of the mustard seed and the leaven belong to the same category.

First we will look at the story of this parable. Again Jesus tells us about a sower. How does this one act? He first casts his seed over the ground and then leaves the field to go home. In the meantime the seed *grows by itself*, and then gradually fruit comes forth, "first the blade, then the ear, afterwards the full corn in the ear." And then the sower returns to the field and "immediately he putteth in the sickle, because the harvest is come." With this saying by the Prophet Joel (4:13) Jesus ends this short parable. What is its lesson? The kingdom of God does not come in the near future, as some of those around Jesus had presumed (see Luke 19:11). Rather, the process is very much like the one of the seed in the field. First the seed has to be sown, then the seed must gradually grow, and

only after it has ripened can the harvest begin. In
looking closer at the text of this parable, however,
we find that Jesus does not compare the kingdom
of God with the seed, but with the sower: "So is the
kingdom of God, as if a man should cast seed into
the earth. . . ." And who is meant by the sower in
this religious reality of salvation? Why, of course,
Jesus Himself. The Messias is meant, Whose figure
cannot be separated from the biblical perception of
the kingdom of God. It is the Messias Jesus Who
casts out the seed of God's kingdom; then He re-
tires "into a far country," as it says in the parable
of the pounds (Luke 19:12), but He does not stay
away forever. Instead, He returns with absolute
certainty, namely, when the time of harvest has
come. In the symbolic language of the Bible the
word "harvest" signifies an image of the Last Judgment (here see also Matt. 13:30). The sower who
returns for the "harvest" is thus the Christ of the
Parousia Who sends out His "sickle" (Apoc. 14:14–
16). This is how Jesus speaks in a hidden manner of
His work of salvation. He means: "Rest assured, I
have not only sown the seed but I will return quite
surely when the time of harvest has come." Yet,
the middle part of the parable's story (the quiet,
fairly imperceptible ripening of the fields until harvest time), has a very important function in the lesson of this parable, which implies: Rest assured,
the Sower will return quite certainly, not right after
the time of seeding, but only when the seed has ripened and the time of harvest has come, that is, when

history is ripe for the Parousia of Our Lord (see Jas. 5:7).

Thus the parable of the self-growing seed, chosen to be the last one to end the interpretations of the parables of Jesus, points to the *Returning Lord,* and therefore it is this figure of Him which should fill the Christian's consciousness completely and in that special way Jesus asked for: "And you yourselves (should be) like to men who wait for their lord. . . ." (Luke 12:36).

SUMMARY

The essential themes of these nineteen parables interpreted in this book can be listed as: the reign of God (the kingdom of God), the sentiment of God, conversion, prayer, judgment, religious decision, the neighbor, Israel's lack of faith, and the Second Coming of Jesus.

One of the main themes is the eschatological reign of God which begins forcefully with the appearance of the Messianic Sower in Galilee, though the final manifestation of that reign is yet to come. This reign is the most precious thing man can discover. Through its announcement by the Messianic Sower, an eschatological event has been inaugurated which cannot be arrested and which, ultimately, after the manifestation of God's reign at the end of time, will overshadow and penetrate everything. For the time being, the enemy is still at work till the great separation will take place on the day of harvest. A radical decision is necessary to assure oneself of one's eschatological existence and of a conversion in good time—another important theme of the parables of Jesus—a decision which is the most important precondition for a participation in the banquet of God's kingdom. Even sinners are not excluded therefrom, much to the annoyance of overpious men, as long as they return with sincere hearts to the Father. Man should not wallow in the luxuries of life but should rather be constantly prepared for the hour in which God may call him, and he should ready himself with special care to receive the returning Lord because, if he fails to do so, he would knock in vain at a closed door. The call of Jesus for conversion was primarily directed to Israel, the vineyard of God, but this call does not seem to bring forth fruits of repentance, and the spiritual leaders of Israel resemble moody and obstinate children who do not recognize the hour of God which began with Jesus; instead, they harden themselves completely and kill the last messenger of God, His own Son.

*   *   *

Thus, the parables of Jesus announce the last *period of time,* though nothing in them is said about its duration or the fixed day upon which this time of probation will end. That hour remains entirely uncertain. However, the future is sure to bring us the kingdom of God and its advent will begin with a severe judgment by the returned Sower. Thoughts circling around judgment time play a very definite role in the parables of Jesus. This is why there is a continously repeated and almost threatening call to repentance, because, if this repentance shall be lacking, nobody will be justified by God.

The fate of Jesus is scarcely mentioned in these parables. The parable of the wicked tenants in the vineyard is the only one which stresses this point clearly. As the last messenger is killed by the tenants, we can certainly see in this incident a prophetic allusion to the violent death of Jesus. But neither the importance of salvation as a result of this death nor the resurrection from the dead of Him Who was murdered is touched upon, and there is a slight hint of Christ's glorification only in the parable of the entrusted money. Yet, Jesus speaks very clearly of His return in His parables, mostly in connection with thoughts concerning the Last Judgment. This fact corresponds, without doubt, to His other claims about Himself and His desire to be identified as the "Son of man." Obviously the themes used in the parables of Jesus are not specifically "Christian," which proves that they were poorly revised in their "post-Easter" tradition.

The greater part of the parables of Jesus, as evidenced by its themes, was addressed to the *general public* and not to the esoteric circle of His disciples, and only the evangelistic tradition is responsible for any changes made here and there regarding His audience (see introduction). This confirms a pronouncement of the gospel that Jesus spoke to the multitudes in *parables*, and "without parable he did not speak unto them" (Mark 4:33 f.).

BIBLIOGRAPHY

Contributions by the Author for the Interpretation of the Parables

The concept of "neighbor" as proclaimed by Jesus (for the parable of the compassionate samaritan): from the *Theological Magazine of Trier*, No. 64 (1955), pp. 91–99.

Interpretation of Parables and History of Salvation

Applied to the parable of the self-growing seed (Mark 4:26–29): *ibid.*, No. 64 (1955), pp. 257–266.

The Parable of the Severe Miller (Luke 13:22–30)

Contribution to the editing and theology of St. Luke: *ibid.*, No. 65 (1956), pp. 129–143.

The Unheeded Kairos

(Matt. 11:16–19; Luke 7:31–35): *Biblica*, No. 40 (1959), pp. 599–612.

I Q (umran) Hodajoth and the Parable of the Mustard Seed

(Mark 4:30–32 Par.): *Biblical Paper*, NF 3 (1960), pp. 128–130.